Bounti

Grandpa's Handmade Gifts

Authored by

Ulysses S. Moore

Created by

Larry Keith Kirkenslager

Contributions by

Andrea Kirkenslager
Julie Kirkenslager
Tom Carns

Consultant Editor

Marilyn McLeod

Bountiful Season:
Grandpa's Handmade Gifts

Library of Congress Catalog Card Number

International Standard Book Number
978-1499759037

Printed in the United States of America.

Contents

In 1945 I can be seen in the homemade swing made by my Grandpa Moore. His wife Nettie looks on.

Foreword

My grandfather on my mother's side, Ulysses S. Moore, was a renaissance man for his time. Not only did he maintain the family homestead for future generations, he raised his children there, and still managed to make intricate wood carvings, build furniture, and even write and publish poetry. He did all of this in the Midwestern tradition of self-reliance. He didn't email his Word doc of poetry to his local Kinkos, and then pick up the finished product at the local counter. Instead he typeset every letter of every poem and created the finished product on his own manual printing press upstairs in his attic.

I was the grandson who lived next door and was called upon to help him. This was the early 1950s in the Midwest, in the rural countryside of Illinois in the hills overlooking the Mississippi river. As I look back it was sort of a primitive childhood. I remember how things changed when I was in the fifth grade. I watched as power lines were installed from the power grid in the city, down the gravel road leading to our house. Before that in the winter time we had only wood heating stoves in the homes, and kerosene lamps for light ... no electricity.

This violin was made by U.S. Moore in 1955 when he was 90 years old. It was made from wood cut from the timber on his homestead.

My grandfather and grandmother lived in their home on top of a hilly area of our family homestead. Between their home and our home was the barn and the barn lot. Surrounding our house we had about two acres that bordered the fields, and contained our house, garage, chicken house, outhouse, and a garden behind the house.

Our water came from two sources: a pitcher pump in the kitchen drawing from a cistern in the ground below the house for wash water, and a water pump outside for drinking water. We'd get water from the outside pump, and keep a pail of clean water in the pantry with a dipper. The procedure involved using the handle on the pump as a lever, moving it up and down fast enough to encourage the water in the earth below to eventually come to the surface, and finally pour out of the pump into the pail waiting beneath the spigot. The dipper was used by family members to drink water from the pail.

I didn't mind helping my grandfather. It was just part of the way I grew up in rural Illinois. My grandparents worked hard, and I worked hard. The culture supported respect for your elders. The chores given to me in my early years established a work ethic that continues to this day.

Crescent School 1950 grade 1 when I was 6 years old. My grandfather built this one room country school in Illinois. Terry Carpenter and I are in the front row.

One winter my grandmother hurt her ankle and couldn't get around well enough to do her normal work. My grandfather was about 90 years old at the time. As the grandson next door, I was assigned extra duties to help out. I was in the first grade, between six to seven years old. Each morning I would fill the wood box up, get in two buckets of coal, and prepare my grandparents a breakfast of two poached eggs, oatmeal and sassafras tea.

After chores I walked the two miles to the one room country schoolhouse which my grandfather built for the community. There were six students in my entire school at the time. The local Carpenter family had eight children, four of which attended school with me: Benny, Gloria, David and Terry Carpenter. Kay Hafferty and I filled out the rest of the student body. My siblings had already graduated. I was the youngest left at home. By fifth grade we were up to nine students. Kay and Gloria had graduated, but we had gained Thomas Edmunds, Sheldon, Carol, Betty and George Reynolds, and Larry Sandberg.

The school, as our homes, was heated with a wood stove. At home there was a wood cook stove in the kitchen. The split wood logs that filled the wood box would be taken from the wood stacked outside. A watchful eye was kept on the fire at all times, to make sure the house continued to stay warm. Once the fire had died down and it was time to re-stoke the fire, a lump of coal was added to the bottom of the stove first, then wood on top. The coals kept the heat radiating to the house longer after the wood on top had burned to ash.

Crescent School 1952 grade 3. I am in the middle of the back row in front of the teacher.

My grandparents' and my own parents' homes were designed in a similar way, though my grandparents' home was larger. My grandfather had built them both as rambling homes with a second story. Downstairs was the kitchen, pantry, living room, and the downstairs bedroom where the parents slept. I had the bedroom upstairs. In order to conserve heat in the winter, all areas of the house except the kitchen, pantry and the downstairs bedroom were closed off, to provide a smaller area to heat. There was no heat in the upstairs bedroom. In order to stay warm, I had to rely on heat that would rise from the kitchen downstairs through the grate in the floor of my bedroom.

There was no bathroom inside the house. We did our business in the outhouse which was located about 120 feet from the front door of our house. In winter we made a path to the outhouse through the snow. An outhouse was a small wooden structure built over a deep pit dug into the ground. Inside was a platform at the height of a chair, with a hole cut into the horizontal board where one sat. The holes were large enough to provide clear access to the hole beneath, but small enough to provide support so one didn't fall in. The number of holes in the platform would give it the 'model' type: one-holer, three-holer, etc. This could mean you might share the experience with a friend or family member.

Our old newspapers and Sears catalogs would sit in stacks on the platform next to us, to be used as toilet paper. My more modern family also had toilet paper. My grandfather had a fancier looking outhouse, and when I first used it I noticed two kettles of corn cobs next to the newspaper. One kettle was filled with red corn cobs, and the other kettle was filled with white corn cobs. When I asked him what these were for, he explained I should use the red corn cob for the first pass, and the white corn cob to check for anything left.

This worked fine during the day, however at night as the fire in the wood stoves burned down and provided less radiant heat, the rooms inside the house would get colder, and of course it was even colder outside. We kept a white porcelain pot with a lid on the back porch which was emptied into the outhouse every morning, but it was preferable to take care of business before going to bed if possible, since getting out from under the blanket, finding one's by then cold shoes, and creeping down the stairs through the now-cold house to the even-colder back porch, made trying to go back to sleep instead more attractive.

In the morning the rooster would crow at first light and wake us up. I would get dressed, eat breakfast, then do my chores and walk to school. The work day for each of us would begin all over again. In his younger years, my grandfather would have begun working the fields, but he was now retired. My parents leased our fields to other farmers, and my father worked in the city thirteen miles away in Iowa, in a boiler factory.

When I was about twelve years old I began working for other farmers in the summer time. I sometimes fed pigs, cultivated corn, and did other normal farm chores. One farmer had a business going from farm to farm doing custom bailing. He would have me ride the rack (a platform on wheels made to be pulled behind a tractor). I would stack bails of hay onto the rack as they came off the bailer.

The bailer was a piece of farm machinery, also made to be pulled behind a tractor, that would take the dried stalks of hay, alfalfa, corn or grains (after the edible parts of the plants had been harvested, the stems cut and dried, and then rolled into windrows), and press the stems into compact rectangular cubes called bails. Once the dried stems were rolled into windrows in the field, and the field was dry, a farmer would bring his tractor to where his machinery was stored and first hook up the bailer, then an empty rack behind the bailer. Then the tractor would pull both bailer and rack to the edge of the field ready to be harvested.

My grandfather built this desk from an oak tree on our farm. It sits in my home today as a centerpiece to the entryway.

One man would drive and guide the tractor so the bailer would be correctly positioned to pick up the dried stems waiting in the windrow, and other man (me) would catch each bail as it came out of the bailer, and stack it in place on the rack. When the rack was full it was disconnected from the bailer, and replaced with an empty rack. The full rack would be pulled to the barn by another man on a tractor where other people were waiting to 'mow' the bails, meaning move the bails from the rack into the barn, or the hay mow. There they would be stored until needed for various uses on the farm.

One of the chores a farmer's wife had was to feed the crew. If the field was close to the house, at lunch time she might call out and wave to the men in the field, telling them it was time for lunch. Or she might pack a lunch for each man and send the children out to bring the men their meal. Jugs of water were often left at the ends of the field rows, especially when manual work was done, such as hoeing weeds that few up among the crops while the plants were still fairly young.

As my grandfather got older he passed on maintenance of his fields to others, and spent more of his time making intricate wood carvings. He would take a solid piece of wood and carve continuous chains. He also made a big ornamental clock face and several pieces of furniture. The desk in the picture to the left was made from an oak tree on our farm. My grandfather cut down the tree, sawed the tree into logs, had the logs cut into boards, and then fashioned the desk himself. He had a big saw that was run by a gasoline motor on a pulley. The motor ran the belt with a shiv that started and ran the saw.

I would go over to visit my grandfather, as most kids do, because there were no other kids around. I would watch him doing his chores or his projects, and we'd talk. He read the Bible a lot. One day I arrived and didn't find my grandfather right away, so I asked my grandmother where he was. She told me he was up in a little room upstairs.

It was hot that summer, and I found him way upstairs in a small room with the windows closed. There he was with his printing press, setting type. He showed me how to help him. He had a poem he had written on a piece of paper, and a wood block and a tray of individual metal letters in front of him. With a tweezers he would pick up one letter at a time, and insert it into the wood block to 'type' out each line of his poem. This had to be 'written' into the block backwards, so the finished type on the paper would come out readable. For each poem we would make a new block of intricately arranged metal letters, because each poem was different.

When he had all the individual metal letters arranged the way he wanted them on a block, he would secure it with something like a vice grip so the pieces wouldn't shift when he placed it on the printing press.

The wheel of the printing press was round. My grandfather would take a paint pan and roll ink on the wheel, then pull down the lever to press the inked block against the paper. The trick was to get just enough ink on the letters in the block, so each letter was reproduced unto the paper clearly, and not so much ink that the letters would bleed into each other. When you see a missing letter, or one letter upside down, remember a 90 year old man used a tweezers to set each individual letter row by row in a small wooden block to create each page. If you see a comma instead of a period, it's probably because he ran out of periods.

He sent away for the paper, which was made of cotton rags, and came in various colors. Once a sheet of paper was printed and was dry, he'd cut it into the smaller sizes needed for individual pages for the book or calendar. Then he would stitch them together using something like a sewing machine, to keep the pages in order. Sometimes the paper wouldn't be cut exactly straight, or the printing might be a little crooked, or a letter might be upside down, simply indicating the enormous number of detailed steps he took to create the finished product. It was a tedious, arduous task to come up with any type of volume.

In this book you are reading today, my wife Andrea and I have reproduced the four calendars that are left in our home from the many years my grandfather created his calendars, and the thousands of copies that he distributed. Perhaps others who find this book have more copies in their archives, and would be willing to share them with us.

We hope you enjoy my grandfather's poems.

Larry Kirkenslager
Huntington Beach, California
June 6, 2014

Farm home address until 1961

Rural Route 1
Lomax, Illinois

Larry Kirkenslager
May 2014

This is an actual photo of their dog.

Calendar for
1951

Greetings
from
U.S. & Anna Moore
& Their Dog

Lomax, Ill.

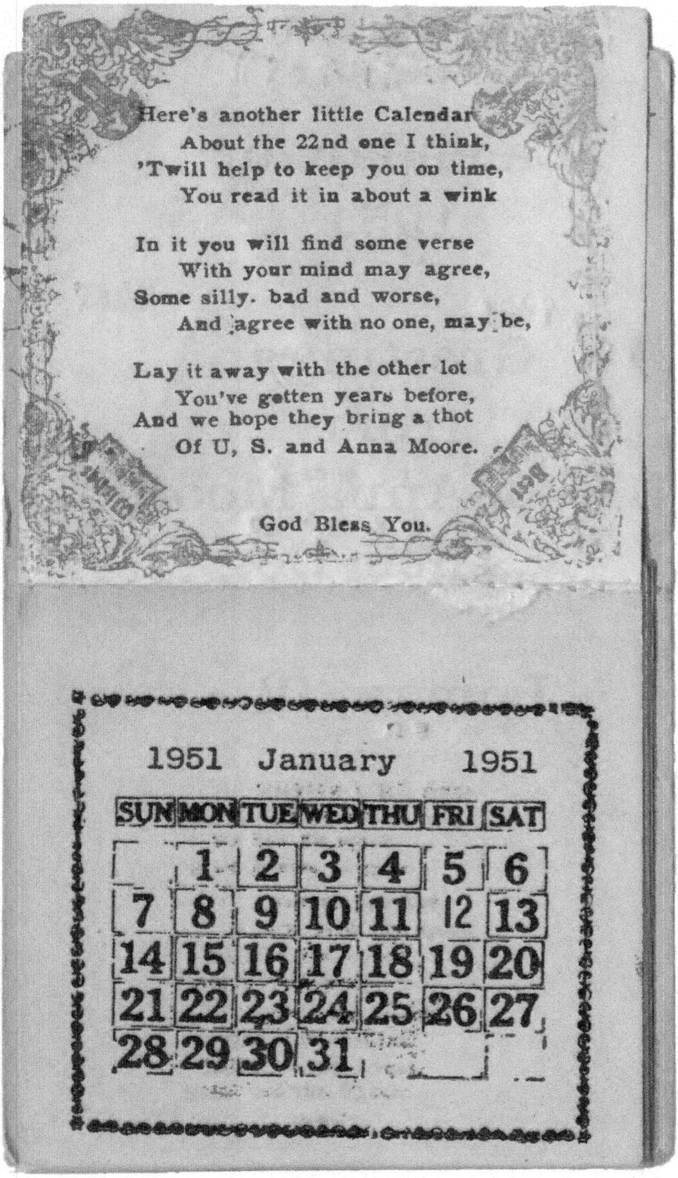

Here's another little Calendar
About the 22nd one I think,
'Twill help to keep you on time,
You read it in about a wink

In it you will find some verse
With your mind may agree,
Some silly. bad and worse,
And agree with no one, may be,

Lay it away with the other lot
You've gotten years before,
And we hope they bring a thot
Of U, S. and Anna Moore.

God Bless You.

1951 January 1951

SUN	MON	TUE	WED	THU	FRI	SAT
	1	2	3	4	5	6
7	8	9	10	11	12	13
14	15	16	17	18	19	20
21	22	23	24	25	26	27
28	29	30	31			

January
1951

Here's another little Calendar
About the 22nd one I think,
'Twill help to keep you on time,
You read it in about a wink

In it you will find some verse
With your mind may agree,
Some silly, bad and worse,
And agree with no one, may be,

Lay it away with the other lot
You've gotten years before,
And we hope they bring a thot
Of U.S. and Anna Moore.

God Bless You.

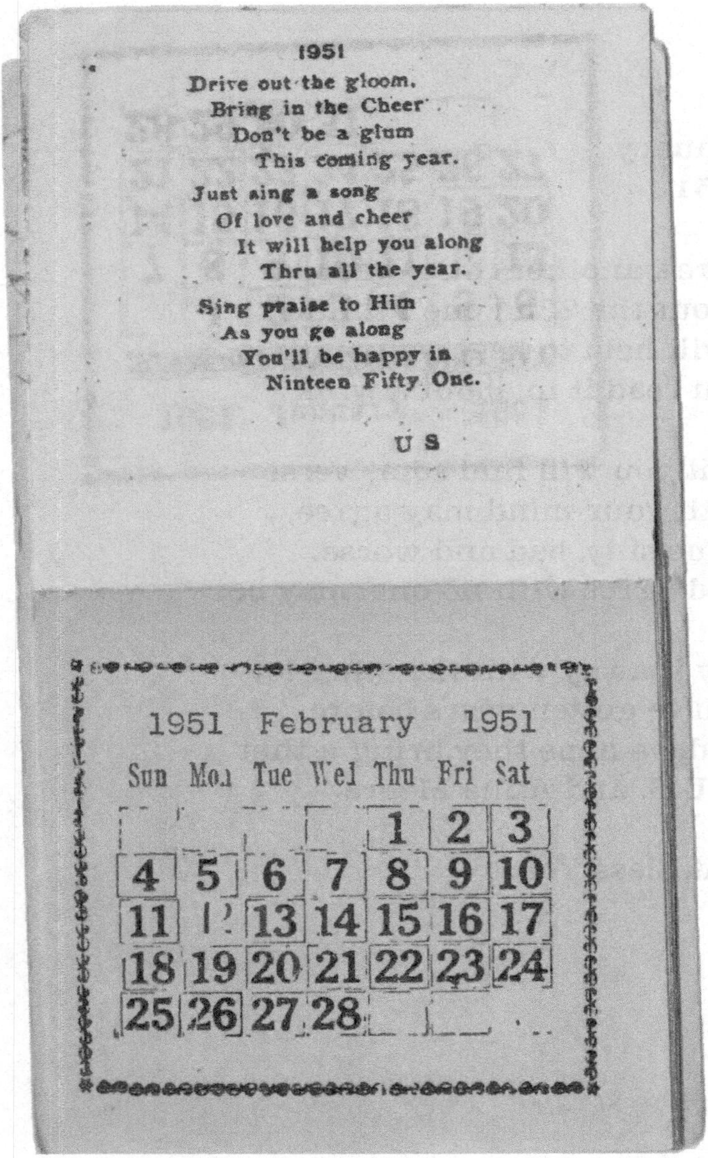

1951

Drive out the gloom,
Bring in the Cheer
Don't be a glum
This coming year.

Just sing a song
Of love and cheer
It will help you along
Thru all the year.

Sing praise to Him
As you go along
You'll be happy in
Ninteen Fifty One.

U S

1951 February 1951

Sun	Mon	Tue	Wed	Thu	Fri	Sat
				1	2	3
4	5	6	7	8	9	10
11	[illegible]	13	14	15	16	17
18	19	20	21	22	23	24
25	26	27	28			

February
1951

Drive out the gloom.
Bring in the Cheer
Don't be a glum
This coming year.

Just sing a song
Of love and cheer
It will help you along
Thru all the year.

Sing praise to Him
As you go along
You'll be happy in
Nineteen Fifty One.

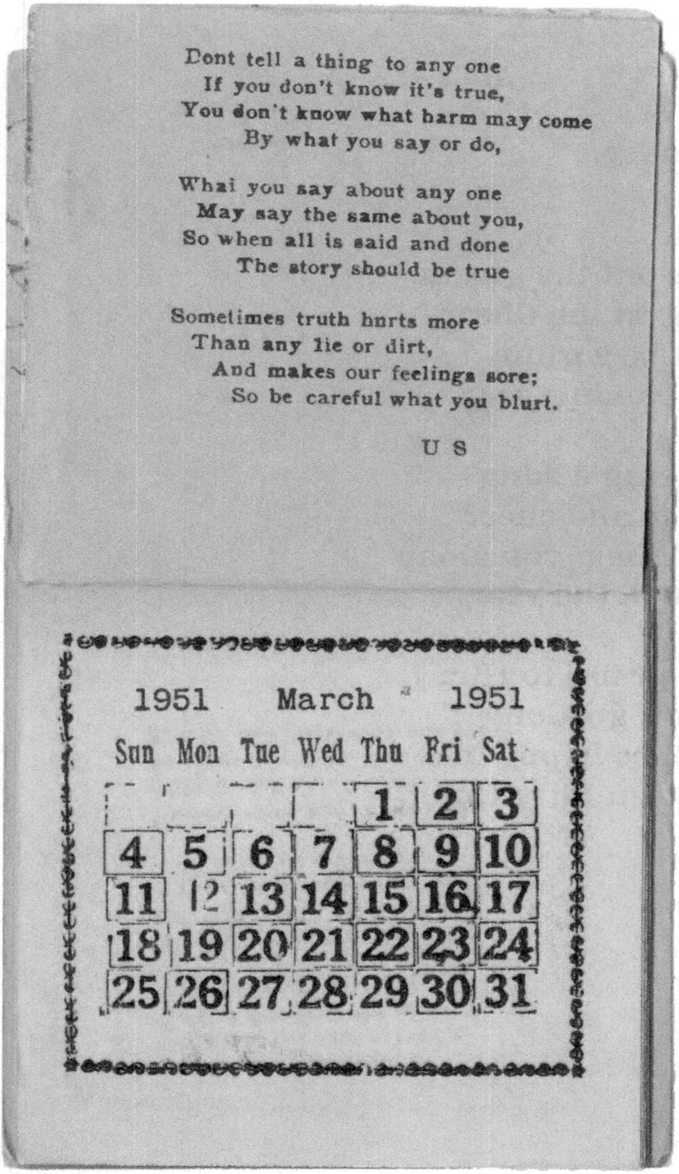

Dont tell a thing to any one
If you don't know it's true,
You don't know what harm may come
By what you say or do,

Whai you say about any one
May say the same about you,
So when all is said and done
The story should be true

Sometimes truth hurts more
Than any lie or dirt,
And makes our feelings sore;
So be careful what you blurt.

U S

1951 March 1951

Sun	Mon	Tue	Wed	Thu	Fri	Sat
				1	2	3
4	5	6	7	8	9	10
11	12	13	14	15	16	17
18	19	20	21	22	23	24
25	26	27	28	29	30	31

March
1951

Don't tell a thing to any one
If you don't know it's true,
You don't know what harm may come
By what you say or do,

What you say about any one
May say the same about you,
So when all is said and done
The story should be true

Sometimes truth hurts more
Than any lie or dirt,
And makes our feeling sore;
So be careful what you blurt.

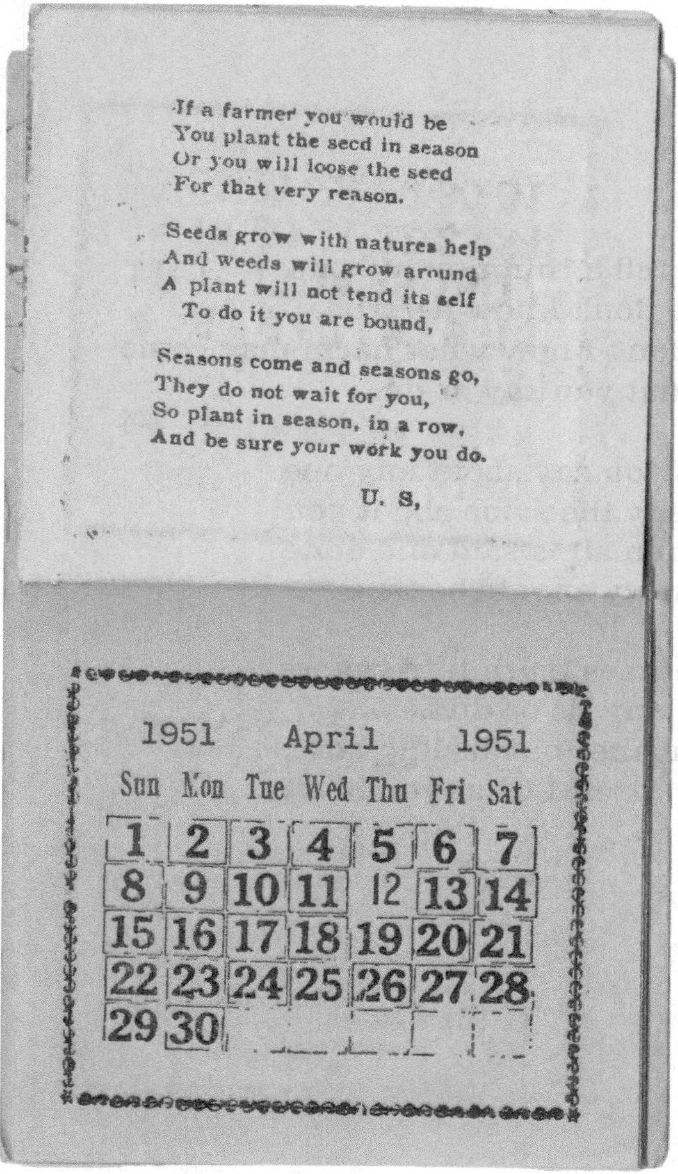

If a farmer you would be
You plant the secd in season
Or you will loose the seed
For that very reason.

Seeds grow with natures help
And weeds will grow around
A plant will not tend its self
To do it you are bound,

Seasons come and seasons go,
They do not wait for you,
So plant in season, in a row,
And be sure your work you do.

U. S,

1951 April 1951

Sun	Mon	Tue	Wed	Thu	Fri	Sat
1	2	3	4	5	6	7
8	9	10	11	12	13	14
15	16	17	18	19	20	21
22	23	24	25	26	27	28
29	30					

April
1951

If a farmer you would be
You plant the seed in season
Or you will loose the seed
For that very reason.

Seeds grow with natures help
And weeds will grow around
A plant will not tend its self
To do it you are bound,

Seasons come and seasons go,
They do not wait for you,
So plant in season, in a row,
And be sure your work you do.

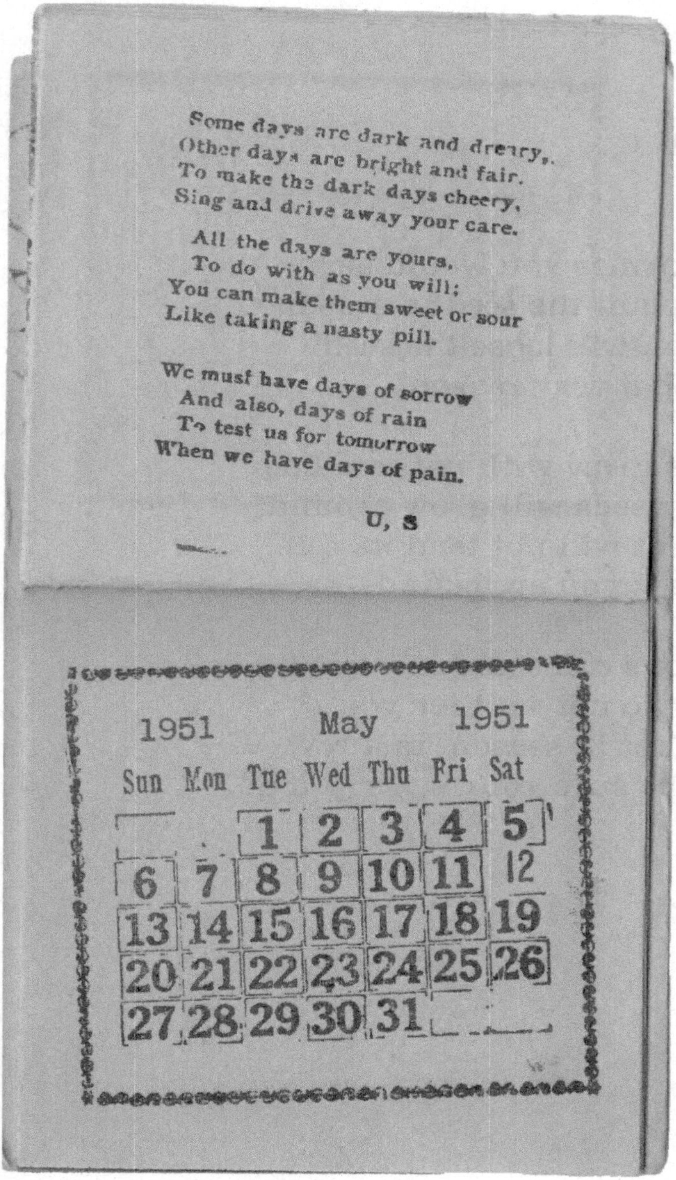

Some days are dark and dreary,
Other days are bright and fair.
To make the dark days cheery,
Sing and drive away your care.

All the days are yours,
To do with as you will;
You can make them sweet or sour
Like taking a nasty pill.

We must have days of sorrow
And also, days of rain
To test us for tomorrow
When we have days of pain.

U, S

1951 May 1951

Sun	Mon	Tue	Wed	Thu	Fri	Sat
		1	2	3	4	5
6	7	8	9	10	11	12
13	14	15	16	17	18	19
20	21	22	23	24	25	26
27	28	29	30	31		

May
1951

Some days are dark and dreary,
Other days are bright and fair.
To make the dark days cheery,
Sing and drive away your care.

All the days are yours,
To do with as you will;
You can make them sweet or sour
Like taking a nasty pill.

We must have days of sorrow
And also, days of rain
To test us for tomorrow
When we have days of pain.

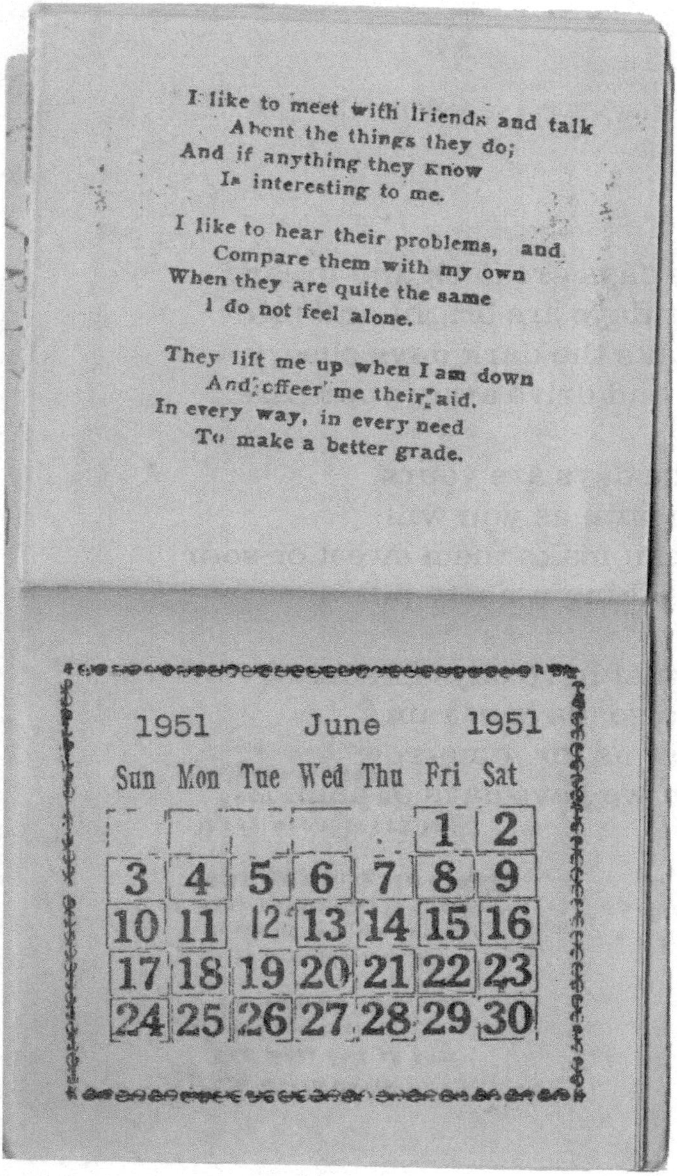

I like to meet with friends and talk
About the things they do;
And if anything they know
Is interesting to me.

I like to hear their problems, and
Compare them with my own
When they are quite the same
I do not feel alone.

They lift me up when I am down
And offeer me their aid.
In every way, in every need
To make a better grade.

1951 June 1951

Sun	Mon	Tue	Wed	Thu	Fri	Sat
					1	2
3	4	5	6	7	8	9
10	11	12	13	14	15	16
17	18	19	20	21	22	23
24	25	26	27	28	29	30

June
1951

I like to meet with friends and talk
About the things they do;
And if anything they know
Is interesting to me.

I like to hear their problems, and
Compare them with my own.
When they are quite the same
I do not feel alone.

They lift me up when I am down
And offer me their aid
In every way, in every need
To make a better grade.

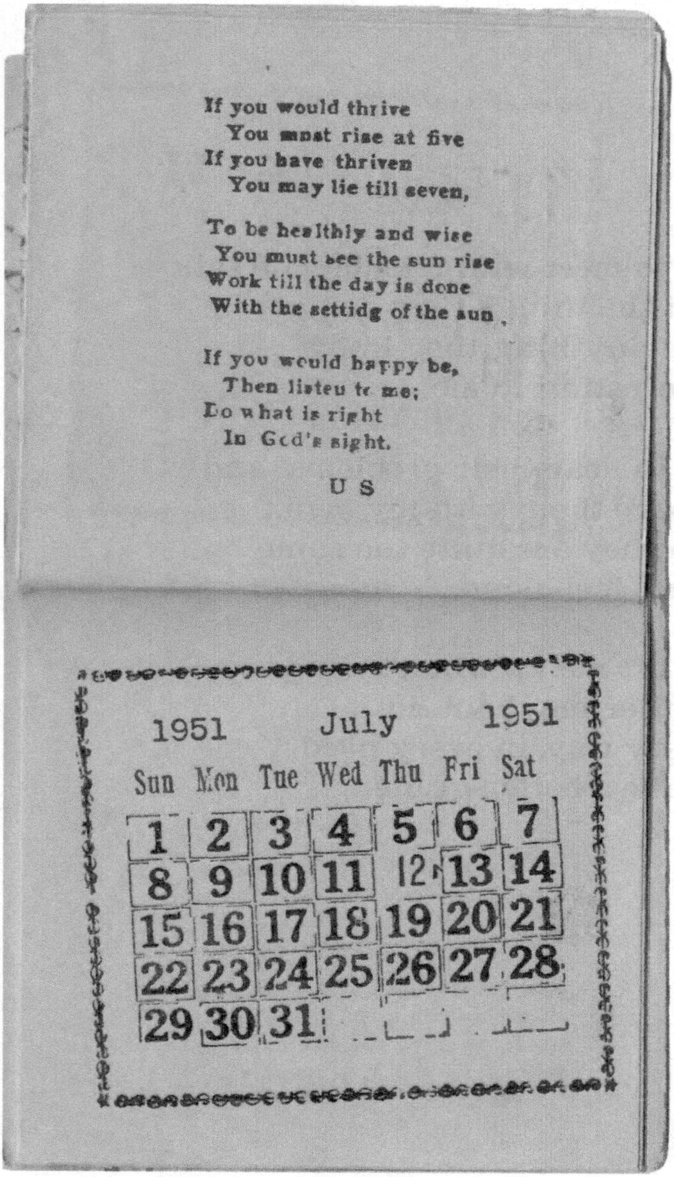

If you would thrive
You must rise at five
If you have thriven
You may lie till seven,

To be healthly and wise
You must see the sun rise
Work till the day is done
With the settidg of the sun.

If you would happy be,
Then listen to me;
Do what is right
In God's sight.

U S

1951 July 1951

Sun	Mon	Tue	Wed	Thu	Fri	Sat
1	2	3	4	5	6	7
8	9	10	11	12	13	14
15	16	17	18	19	20	21
22	23	24	25	26	27	28
29	30	31				

July
1951

If you would thrive
You must rise at five.
If you have thriven
You may lie till seven.

To be healthy and wise
You must see the sun rise
Work till the day is done
With the setting of the sun.

If you would happy be,
Then listen to me;
Do what is right
In God's sight.

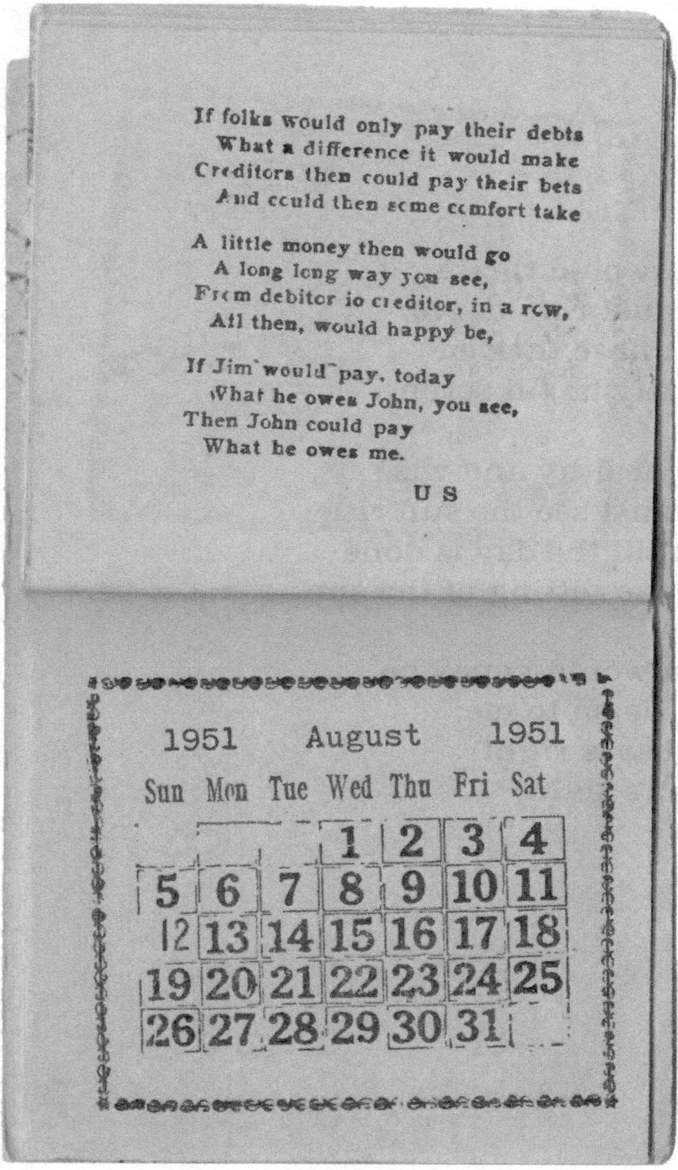
If folks would only pay their debts
What a difference it would make
Creditors then could pay their bets
And could then some comfort take

A little money then would go
A long long way you see,
From debitor to creditor, in a row,
All then, would happy be,

If Jim would pay, today
What he owes John, you see,
Then John could pay
What he owes me.

U S

1951 August 1951

Sun	Mon	Tue	Wed	Thu	Fri	Sat
			1	2	3	4
5	6	7	8	9	10	11
12	13	14	15	16	17	18
19	20	21	22	23	24	25
26	27	28	29	30	31	

August
1951

If folks would only pay their debts
What a difference it would make
Creditors then could pay their bets
And could then some comfort take.

A little money then would go
A long, long way you see,
From debtor to creditor, in a row,
All then, would happy be.

If Jim would pay, today
What he owes John, you see,
Then John could pay
What he owes me.

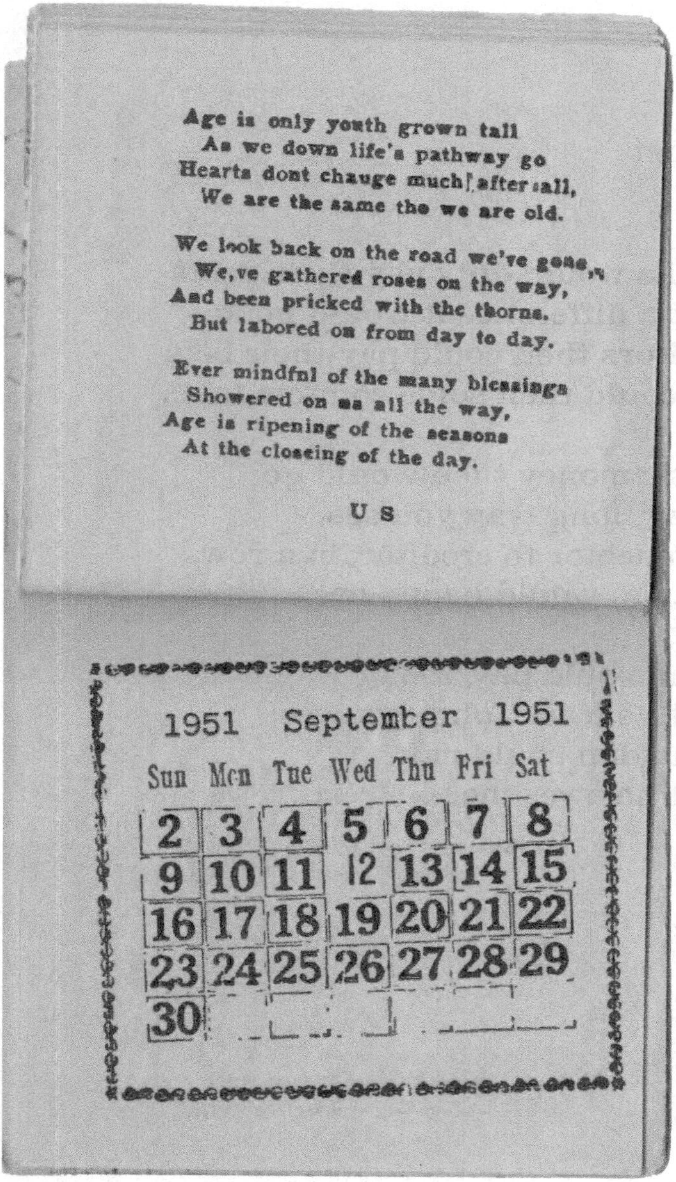

Age is only youth grown tall
As we down life's pathway go
Hearts dont chauge much after all,
We are the same tho we are old.

We look back on the road we've gone,
We,ve gathered roses on the way,
And been pricked with the thorns.
But labored on from day to day.

Ever mindful of the many blessings
Showered on us all the way,
Age is ripening of the seasons
At the closeing of the day.

U S

1951 September 1951

Sun	Mon	Tue	Wed	Thu	Fri	Sat
2	3	4	5	6	7	8
9	10	11	12	13	14	15
16	17	18	19	20	21	22
23	24	25	26	27	28	29
30						

September
1951

Age is only youth grown tall
As we down life's pathway go
Hearts don't change much, after all,
We are the same the we are old.

We look back on the road we've gone,
We've gathered roses on the way,
And been pricked with the thorns,
But labored on from day to day.

Ever mindful of the many blessings
Showered on us all the way,
Age is ripening of the seasons
At the closing of the day.

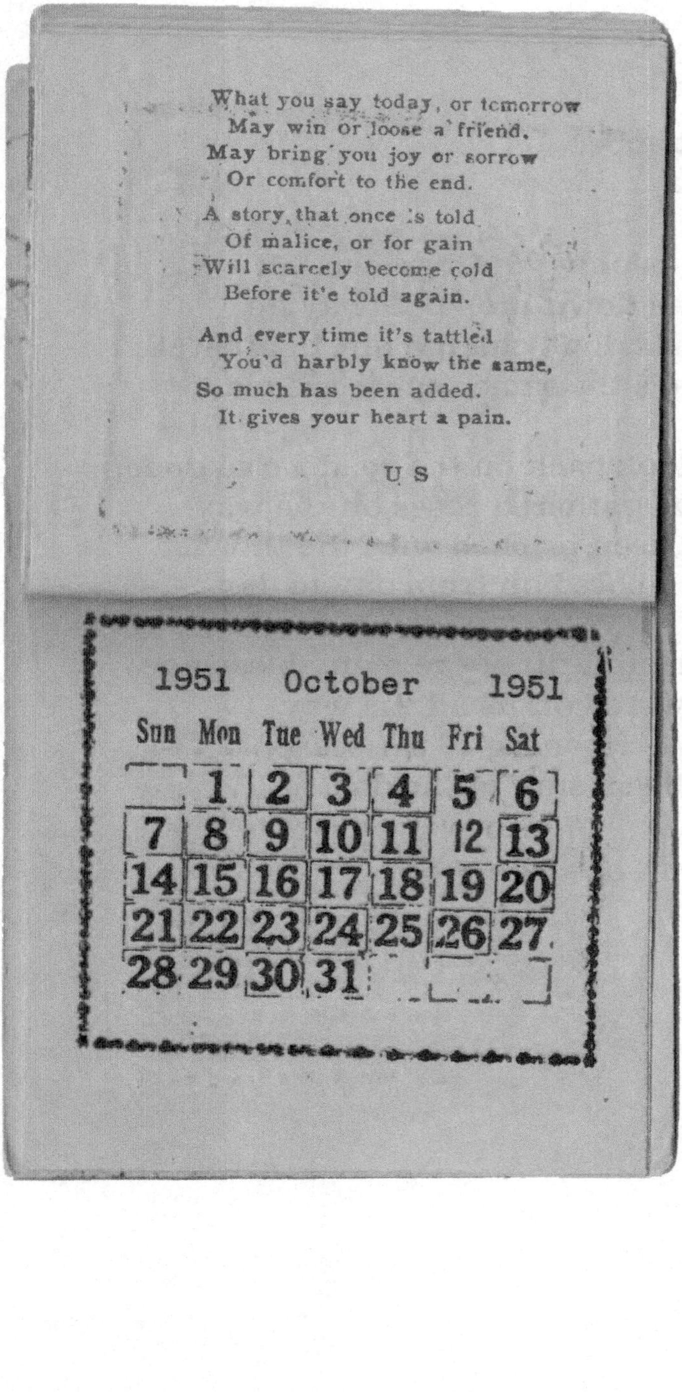

What you say today, or tomorrow
May win or loose a friend,
May bring you joy or sorrow
Or comfort to the end.

A story, that once is told
Of malice, or for gain
Will scarcely become cold
Before it'e told again.

And every time it's tattled
You'd harbly know the same,
So much has been added.
It gives your heart a pain.

U S

1951 October 1951

Sun	Mon	Tue	Wed	Thu	Fri	Sat
	1	2	3	4	5	6
7	8	9	10	11	12	13
14	15	16	17	18	19	20
21	22	23	24	25	26	27
28	29	30	31			

October
1951

What you say today, or tomorrow
May win or loose a friend,
May bring you joy or sorrow
Or comfort to the end.

A story that once is told
Of malice, or for gain
Will scarcely become cold
Before it's told again.

And every time it's tattled
You'd hardly know the same
So much has been added,
It gives your heart a pain.

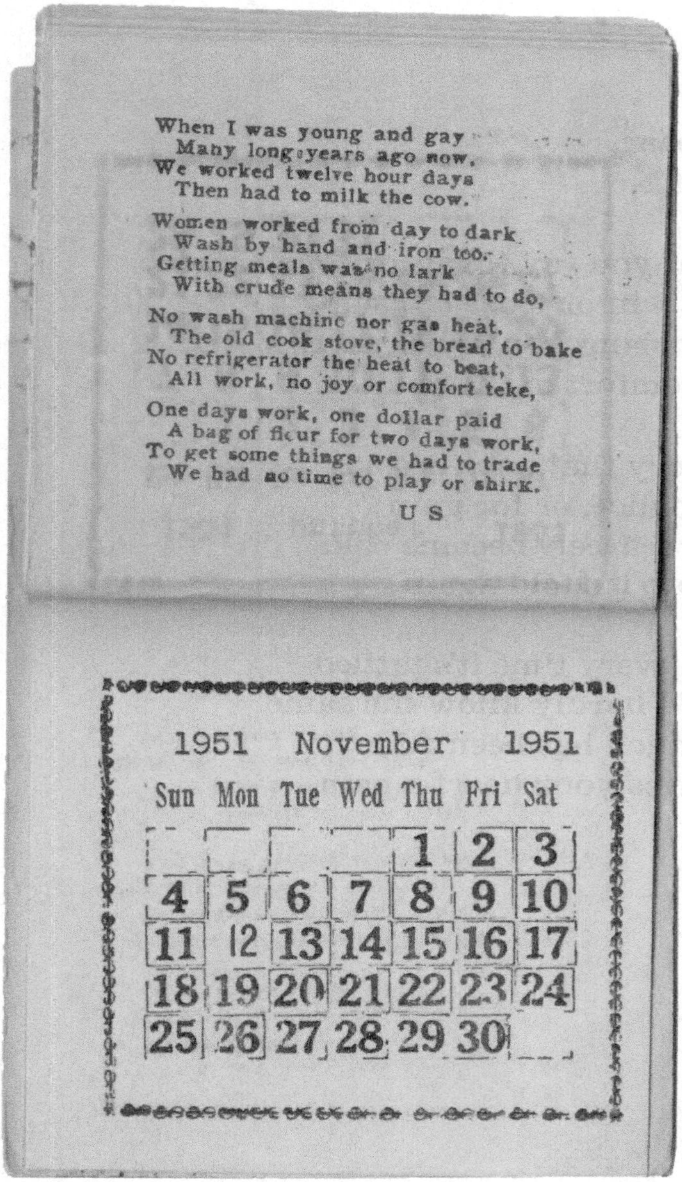
When I was young and gay
  Many long years ago now,
We worked twelve hour days
  Then had to milk the cow.

Women worked from day to dark
  Wash by hand and iron too,
Getting meals was no lark
  With crude means they had to do,

No wash machine nor gas heat,
  The old cook stove, the bread to bake
No refrigerator the heat to beat,
  All work, no joy or comfort teke,

One days work, one dollar paid
  A bag of flour for two days work,
To get some things we had to trade
  We had no time to play or shirk.

U S

1951 November 1951

Sun	Mon	Tue	Wed	Thu	Fri	Sat
				1	2	3
4	5	6	7	8	9	10
11	12	13	14	15	16	17
18	19	20	21	22	23	24
25	26	27	28	29	30	

November
1951

When I was young and gay
Many long years ago now,
We worked twelve hour days
Then had to milk the cow.

Women worked from day to dark
Wash by hand and iron too.
Getting meals was no lark
With crude means they had to do.

No wash machine or gas heat.
The old cook stove, the bread to bake.
No refrigerator the heat to beat,
All work, no joy or comfort take.

One days work, one dollar paid.
A bag of flour for two days work.
To get some things we had to trade.
We had no time to play or shirk.

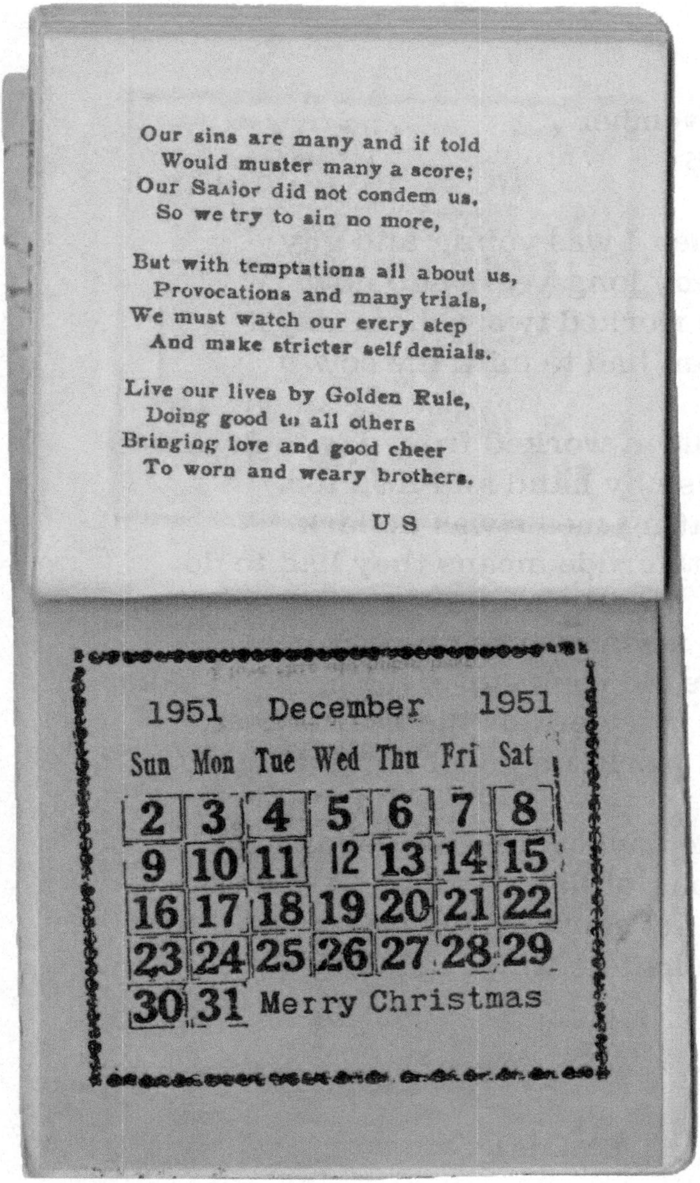

Our sins are many and if told
Would muster many a score;
Our Saʌior did not condem us,
So we try to sin no more,

But with temptations all about us,
Provocations and many trials,
We must watch our every step
And make stricter self denials.

Live our lives by Golden Rule,
Doing good to all others
Bringing love and good cheer
To worn and weary brothers.

U S

1951 December 1951

Sun	Mon	Tue	Wed	Thu	Fri	Sat
2	3	4	5	6	7	8
9	10	11	12	13	14	15
16	17	18	19	20	21	22
23	24	25	26	27	28	29
30	31	Merry Christmas				

December
1951

Our sins are many and if told
Would muster many a score;
Our Savior did not condemn us,
So we try to sin no more.

But with temptations all about us,
Provocations and many trials,
We must watch our every step
And make stricter self denials.

Live our lives by Golden Rule,
Doing good to all others
Bringing love and good cheer
To work and weary brothers.

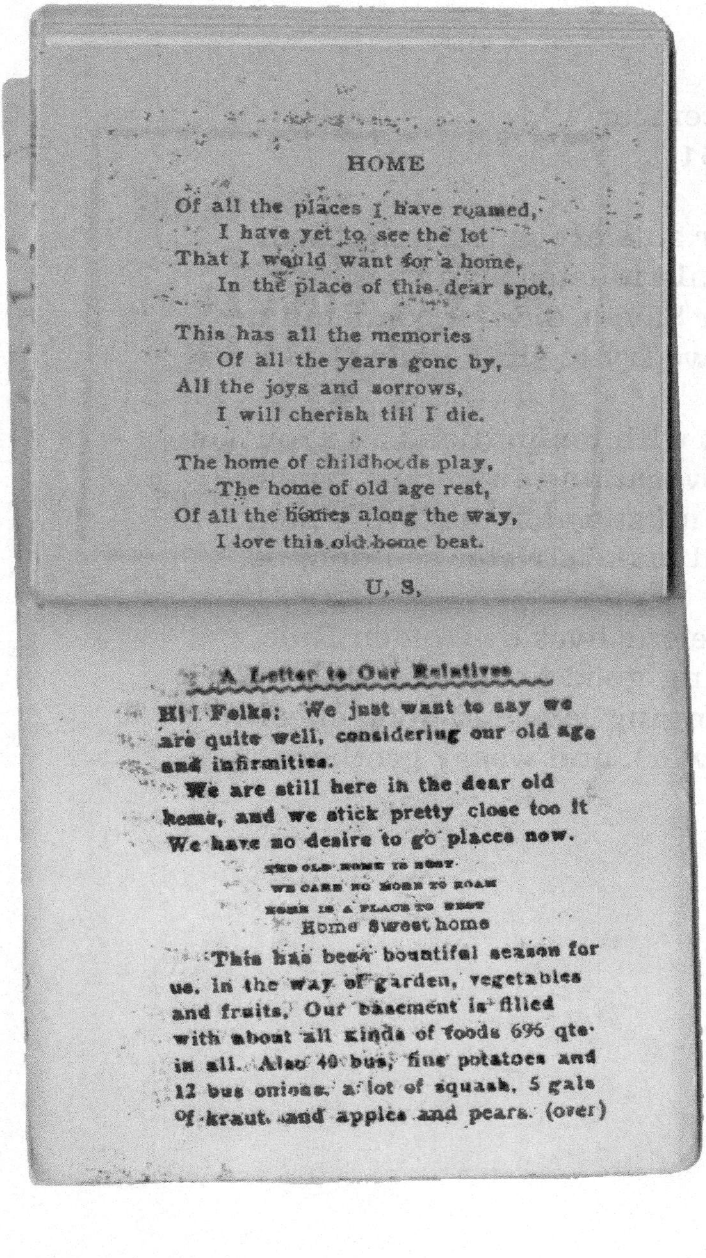

HOME

Of all the places I have roamed,
I have yet to see the lot
That I would want for a home,
In the place of this dear spot.

This has all the memories
Of all the years gone by,
All the joys and sorrows,
I will cherish till I die.

The home of childhoods play,
The home of old age rest,
Of all the homes along the way,
I love this old home best.

U, S,

A Letter to Our Relatives

Hi! Folks: We just want to say we are quite well, considering our old age and infirmities.

We are still here in the dear old home, and we stick pretty close too it We have no desire to go places now.

THE OLD HOME IS BEST
WE CARE NO MORE TO ROAM
HOME IS A PLACE TO REST
Home Sweet home

This has been bountiful season for us, in the way of garden, vegetables and fruits, Our basement is filled with about all kinds of foods 696 qts. in all. Also 40 bus, fine potatoes and 12 bus onions, a lot of squash, 5 gals of kraut, and apples and pears. (over)

HOME
1951

Of all the places I have roamed,
I have yet to see the lot
That I would want for a home,
In the place of this dear spot.

This has all the memories
Of all the years gone by,
All the joys and sorrows
I will cherish till I die.

The home of childhoods play,
The home of old age rest,
Of all the homes along the way,
I love this old home best.

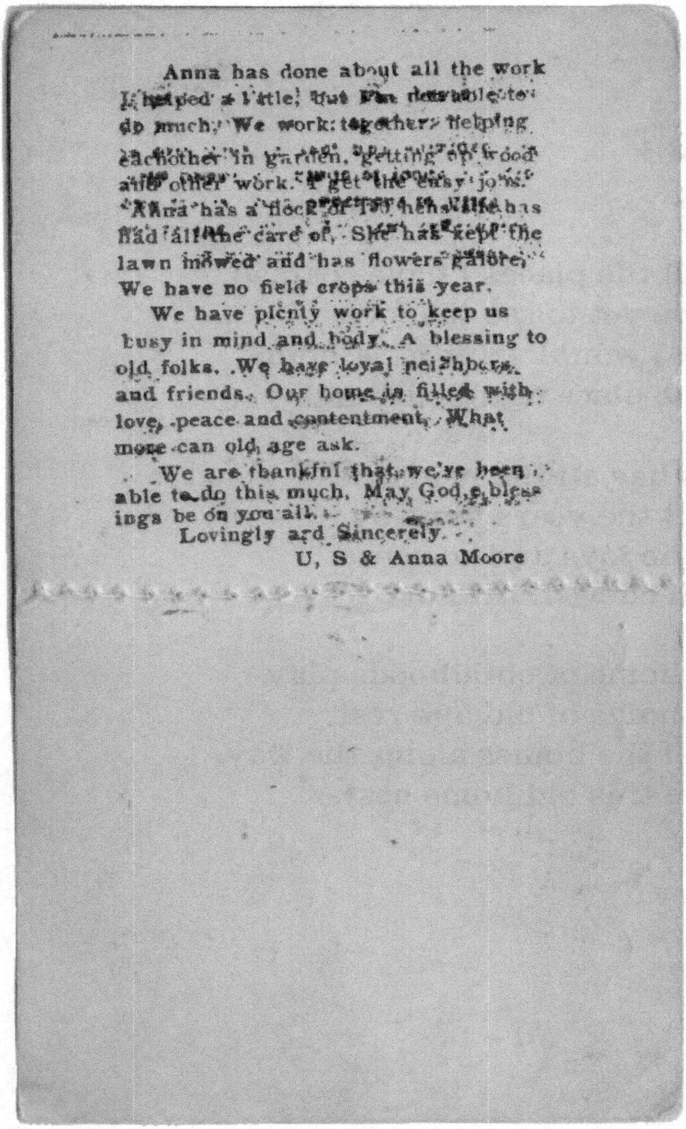

Anna has done about all the work I helped a little, but I'm not able to do much. We work together helping eachother in garden, getting up wood and other work. I get the easy jobs. Anna has a flock of [illegible] hens she has had all the care of. She has kept the lawn mowed and has flowers galore. We have no field crops this year.

We have plenty work to keep us busy in mind and body. A blessing to old folks. We have loyal neighbors and friends. Our home is filled with love, peace and contentment. What more can old age ask.

We are thankful that we've been able to do this much. May God's blessings be on you all.

Lovingly and Sincerely.

U, S & Anna Moore

A Letter to Our Relatives
1951

Hi Folks: We just want to say we
are quite well, considering our old age
and infirmities.

We are still here in the dear old
home, and we stick pretty close to it.
We have no desire to go places now.

The old home is best.
We are no more to roam.
Home is a place to rest.

Home Sweet Home

This has been a bountiful season for
us, in the way of garden, vegetables
and fruits. Our basement is filled
with about all kinds of foods 696 quarts
in all. Also 40 bushels fine potatoes and
12 bushels onions, a lot of squash, 5 gallons
of kraut and apples and pears. (continued)

Anna has done about all the work. I help a little, but was unable to do much. We work together, helping each other in garden, getting up wood and other work. I get the easy jobs. Anna has a flock of hens she has had all the care of. She has kept the lawn mowed and has flowers galore. We have no field crops this year.

We have plenty of work to keep us busy in mind and body. A blessing to old folks. We have loyal neighbors and friends. Our home is filled with love, peace and contentment. What more can old age ask.

We are thankful that we've been able to do this much. May God's blessings be on you all.

Lovingly and Sincerely,
U.S. & Anna Moore

1952

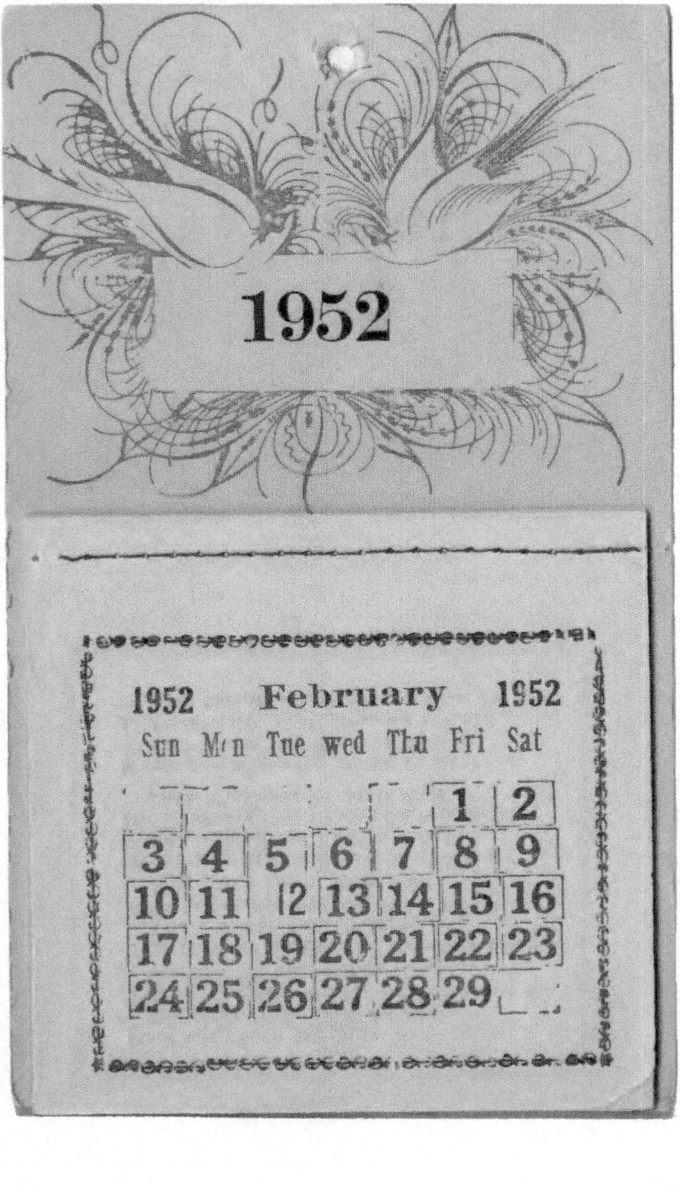
1952
1952 February 1952
Sun Mon Tue Wed Thu Fri Sat
1 2
3 4 5 6 7 8 9
10 11 12 13 14 15 16
17 18 19 20 21 22 23
24 25 26 27 28 29

1952

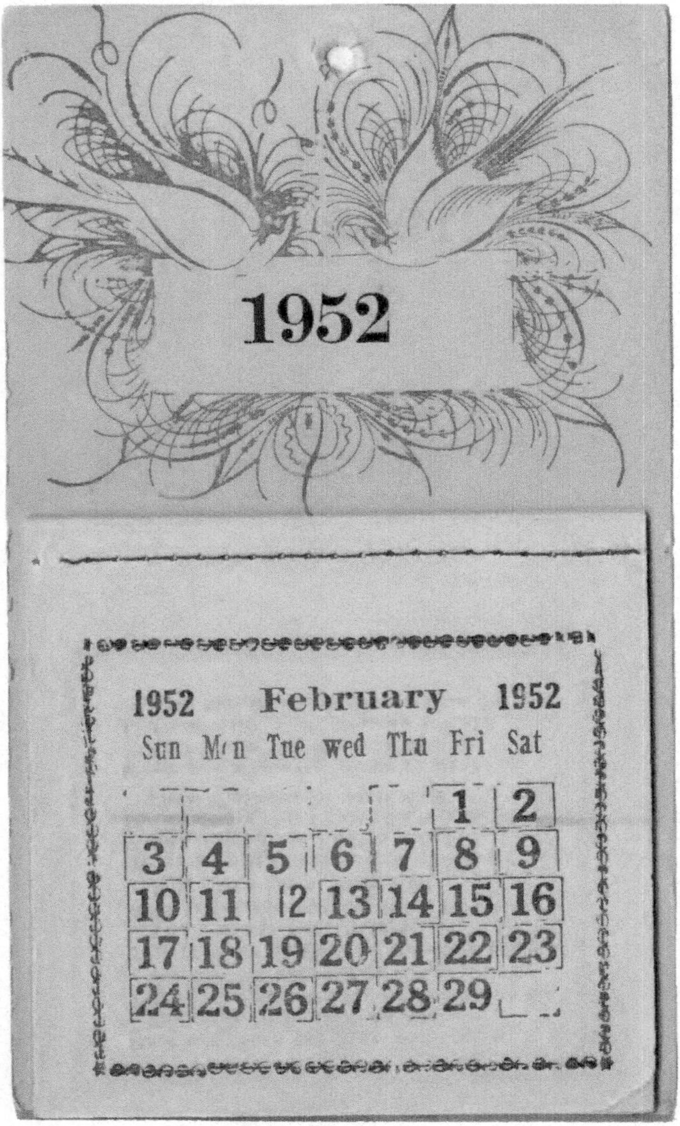
1952
1952 February 1952
Sun Mon Tue wed Thu Fri Sat
1 2
3 4 5 6 7 8 9
10 11 12 13 14 15 16
17 18 19 20 21 22 23
24 25 26 27 28 29

February
1952

The calendar I have begins with February in 1952. January is missing, presumably because we actually used this calendar.

A stamp was used to create the ornate design surrounding '1952'.

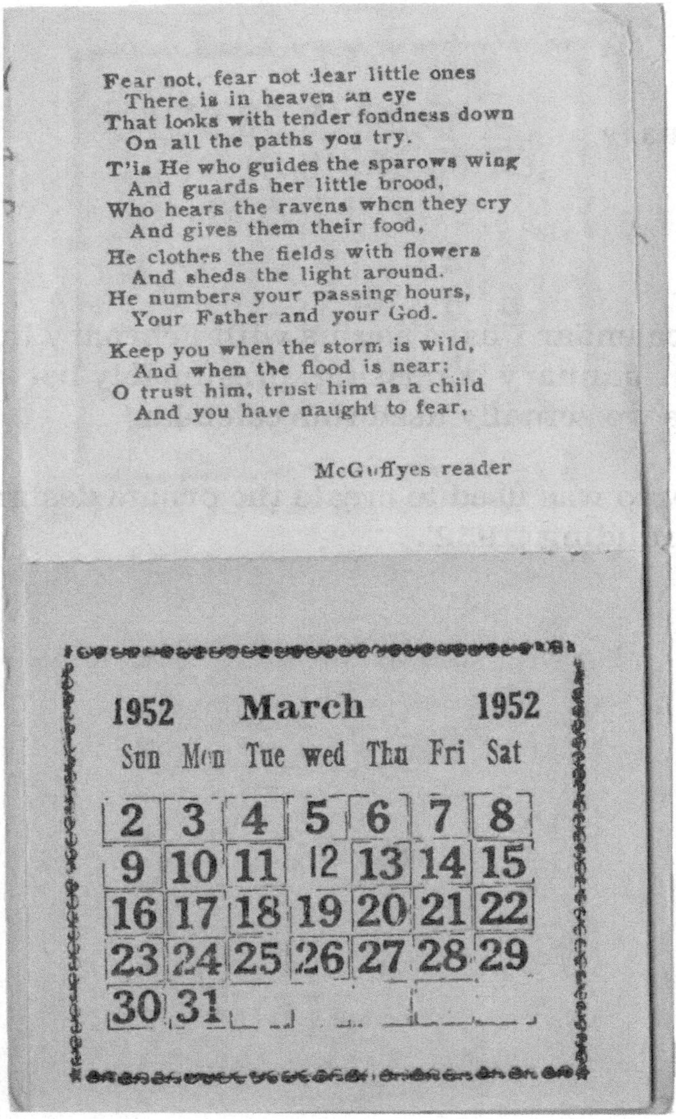

Fear not, fear not dear little ones
There is in heaven an eye
That looks with tender fondness down
On all the paths you try.

T'is He who guides the sparows wing
And guards her little brood,
Who hears the ravens when they cry
And gives them their food,

He clothes the fields with flowers
And sheds the light around.
He numbers your passing hours,
Your Father and your God.

Keep you when the storm is wild,
And when the flood is near;
O trust him, trust him as a child
And you have naught to fear,

McGuffyes reader

1952 March 1952

Sun	Mon	Tue	wed	Thu	Fri	Sat
2	3	4	5	6	7	8
9	10	11	12	13	14	15
16	17	18	19	20	21	22
23	24	25	26	27	28	29
30	31					

March
1952

Fear not, fear not dear little ones.
There is in heaven an eye
That looks with tender fondness down
On all the paths you try.

T'is He who guides the sparrows wing
And guards her little brood,
Who hears the ravens when they cry
And gives them their food.

He clothes the fields with flowers
And sheds the light around.
He numbers your passing hours,
Your Father and your God.

Keep you when the storm is wild,
And when the flood is near;
O trust him, trust him as a child
And you have naught to fear.

McGuffyes reader
(not written by U.S. Moore)

Mary had a little lamb
Its fleece was white as snow
And everywhere that Mary went
The lamd was sure to go.

He followed her to school one day,
Which was against the rule,
Ii made the children laugh and play
To see a lamb at school.

So the teacher turned him out
But still he lingered near
And waited patiently about
Till Mary did appear.

Then he ran to her and laid
His head upon her arm,
As if he said ''I,m not afraid,
You'll keep me from all harm.

Why does the lamb love Mary so?
The eager children cry;
Mary loves the lamb you knew
The teacher did reply.

McGuffeys reader

1952 April 1952

Sun	Mon	Tue	Wed	Thu	Fri	Sat
		1	2	3	4	5
6	7	8	9	10	11	12
13	14	15	16	17	18	19
20	21	22	23	24	25	26
27	28	29	30			

April
1952

Mary had a little lamb
Its fleece was white as snow
And everywhere that Mary went
The lamb was sure to go.

He followed her to school one day,
Which was against the rule.
It made the children laugh and play
To see a lamb at school.

So the teacher turned him out
But still he lingered near
And waited patiently about
Till Mary did appear.

Then he ran to her and laid
His head upon her arm,
As if he said, "I'm not afraid.
You'll keep me from all harm."

Why does the lamb love Mary so?
The eager children cry;
Mary loves the lamb you knew
The teacher did reply.

McGuffeys reader
(not written by U.S. Moore)

Tell me not in mouonful numbers
Life is but an empty dream,
For the soul is dead that slumbers
And things not what they seem.

Life is real, life is earnest
And the grave is not its goal
Dust thou art, to dust returnest,
Was not spoken of the soul.

Not enjoyment, and not sorrow
Is not our destined end or way
But to act that each tomorrow
Find us farther than today.

Lives of great men around us
We can make eur lives sublime,
And, departing, leave behind us
Footprints in the sands of time

Let us then, be up and doing
With a heart for any fate:
Still achieving, and pursuing,
Learm to labor and to wait,

McGuffey reader

1952			May			1952
Sun	Mon	Tue	wed	Thu	Fri	Sat
				1	2	3
4	5	6	7	8	9	10
11	12	13	14	15	16	17
18	19	20	21	22	23	24
25	26	27	28	29	30	31

May
1952

Tell me not in mournful numbers
Life is but an empty dream,
For the soul is dead that slumbers
And things not what they seem.

Life is real, life is earnest
And the grave is not its goal.
Dust thou art, to dust returnest,
Was not spoken of the soul.

Not enjoyment, and not sorrow
Is not our destined end or way
But to act that each tomorrow
Find us farther than today.

Lives of great men around us
We can make our lives sublime,
And, departing, leave behind us
Footprints in the sands of time.

Let us then, be up and doing
With a heart for any fate;
Still achieving, and pursuing,
Learn to labor and to wait.

McGuffey reader
(not written by U.S. Moore)

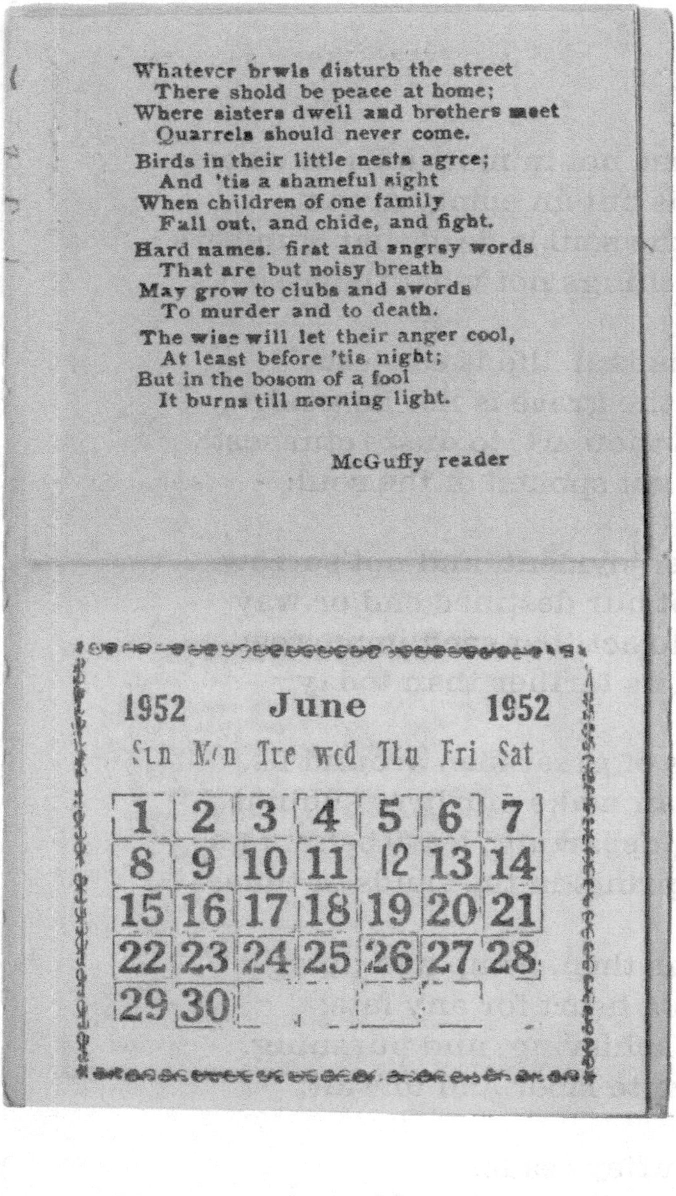

Whatever brwls disturb the street
There shold be peace at home;
Where sisters dwell and brothers meet
Quarrels should never come.

Birds in their little nests agree;
And 'tis a shameful sight
When children of one family
Fall out, and chide, and fight.

Hard names. first and angrsy words
That are but noisy breath
May grow to clubs and swords
To murder and to death.

The wise will let their anger cool,
At least before 'tis night;
But in the bosom of a fool
It burns till morning light.

McGuffy reader

1952 June 1952

Sun	Mon	Tue	Wed	Thu	Fri	Sat
1	2	3	4	5	6	7
8	9	10	11	12	13	14
15	16	17	18	19	20	21
22	23	24	25	26	27	28
29	30					

June
1952

Whatever brawls disturb the street
There should be peace at home;
Where sisters dwell and brothers meet
Quarrels should never come.

Birds in their little nests agree;
And 'tis a shameful sight
When children of one family
Fall out, and chide, and fight.

Hard names, first and angry words
That are but noisy breath
May grow to clubs and swords
To murder and to death.

The wise will let their anger cool,
At least before 'tis night;
But in the bosom of a fool
It burns till morning light.

McGuffey reader
(not written by U.S. Moore)

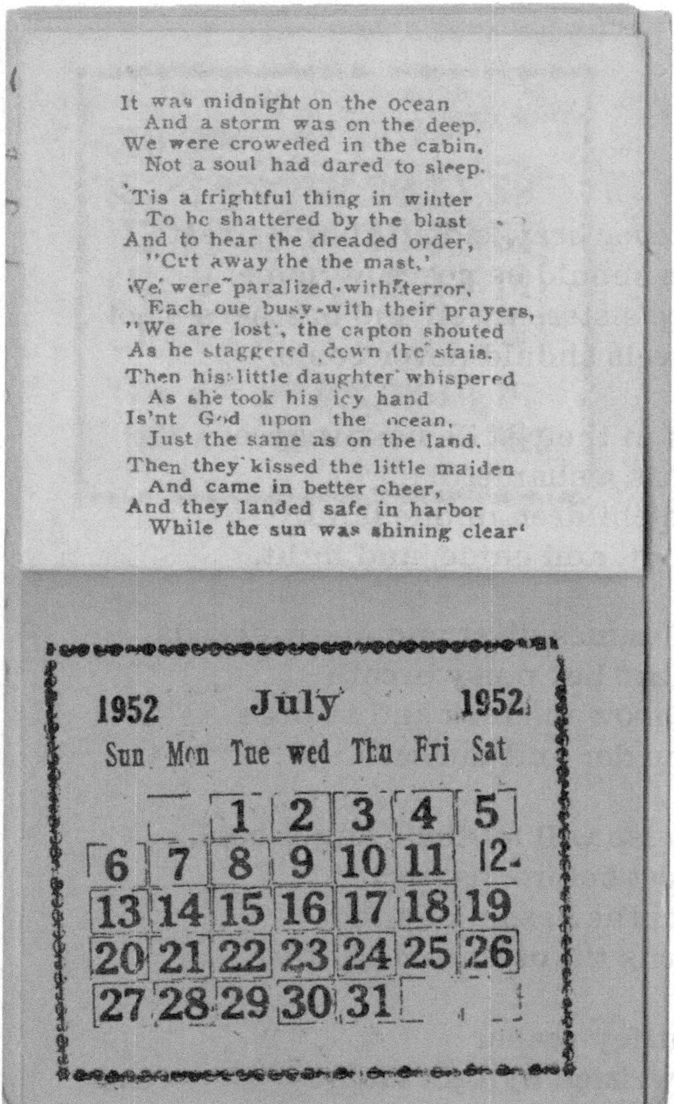

It was midnight on the ocean
And a storm was on the deep.
We were croweded in the cabin,
Not a soul had dared to sleep.

'Tis a frightful thing in winter
To be shattered by the blast
And to hear the dreaded order,
"Cut away the the mast.'

We were paralized with terror,
Each oue busy with their prayers,
"We are lost', the capton shouted
As he staggered down the stais.

Then his little daughter whispered
As she took his icy hand
Is'nt God upon the ocean,
Just the same as on the land.

Then they kissed the little maiden
And came in better cheer,
And they landed safe in harbor
While the sun was shining clear'

1952 July 1952

Sun	Mon	Tue	wed	Thu	Fri	Sat
		1	2	3	4	5
6	7	8	9	10	11	12
13	14	15	16	17	18	19
20	21	22	23	24	25	26
27	28	29	30	31		

July
1952

It was midnight on the ocean
And a storm was on the deep.
We were crowded in the cabin,
Not a soul had dared to sleep.

'Tis a frightful thing in winter
To be shattered by the blast
And to hear the dreaded order,
"Cut away the mast."

We were paralyzed with terror,
Each one busy with their prayers,
"We are lost," the captain shouted
As he staggered down the stairs.

Then his little daughter whispered
As she took his icy hand
Isn't God upon the ocean
Just the same as on the land.

Then they kissed the little maiden
And came in better cheer,
And they landed safe in harbor
While the sun was shining clear.

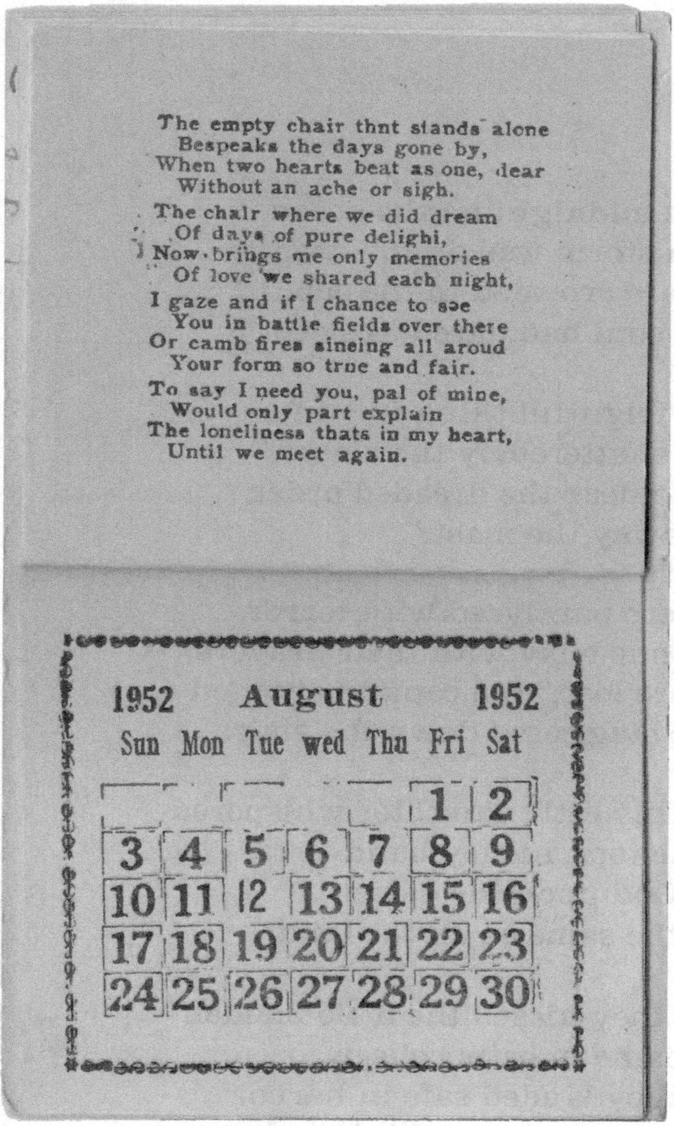
The empty chair thnt stands alone
Bespeaks the days gone by,
When two hearts beat as one, dear
Without an ache or sigh.

The chalr where we did dream
Of days of pure delighi,
Now brings me only memories
Of love we shared each night,

I gaze and if I chance to soe
You in battle fields over there
Or camb fires sineing all aroud
Your form so true and fair.

To say I need you, pal of mine,
Would only part explain
The loneliness thats in my heart,
Until we meet again.

1952 August 1952

Sun	Mon	Tue	wed	Thu	Fri	Sat
					1	2
3	4	5	6	7	8	9
10	11	12	13	14	15	16
17	18	19	20	21	22	23
24	25	26	27	28	29	30

August
1952

The empty chair that stands alone
Bespeaks the days gone by,
When two hearts beat as one, dear
Without an ache or sigh.

The chair where we did dream
of days of pure delight,
Now brings me only memories
Of love we shared each night.

I gaze and if I chance to see
You in battle fields over there
Or camp fires shining all around
Your form so true and fair.

To say I need you, pal of mine,
Would only part explain
The loneliness that's in my heart
Until we meet again.

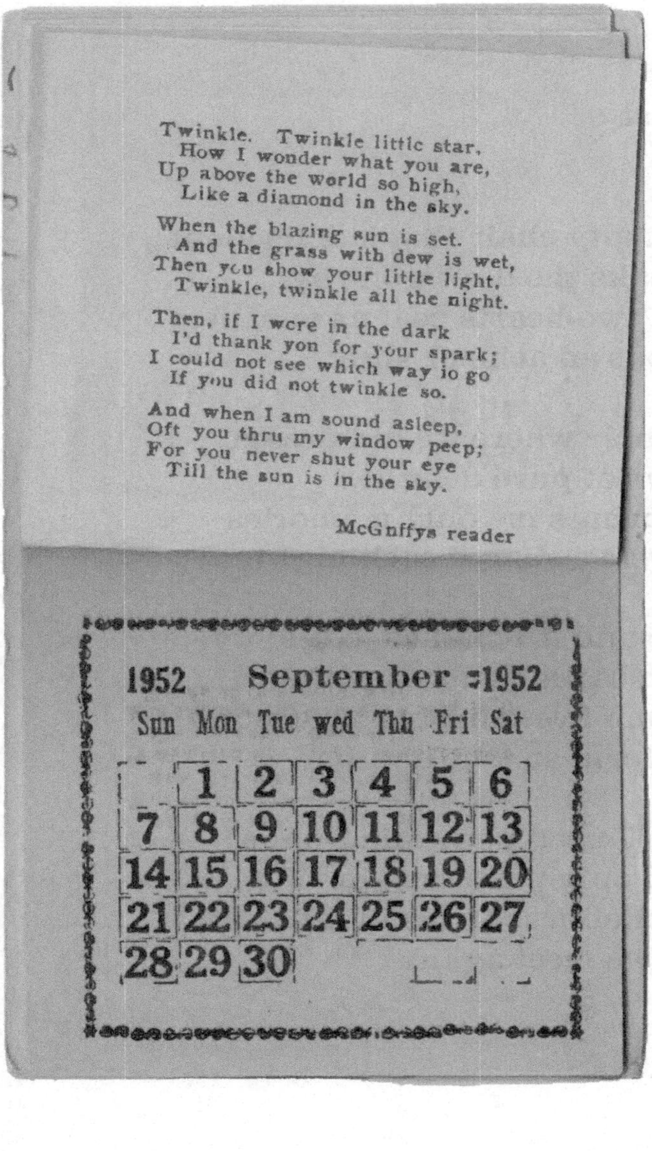

Twinkle. Twinkle little star,
How I wonder what you are,
Up above the world so high,
Like a diamond in the sky.

When the blazing sun is set.
And the grass with dew is wet,
Then you show your little light,
Twinkle, twinkle all the night.

Then, if I were in the dark
I'd thank yon for your spark;
I could not see which way io go
If you did not twinkle so.

And when I am sound asleep,
Oft you thru my window peep;
For you never shut your eye
Till the sun is in the sky.

McGnffys reader

1952 September 1952

Sun	Mon	Tue	wed	Thu	Fri	Sat
	1	2	3	4	5	6
7	8	9	10	11	12	13
14	15	16	17	18	19	20
21	22	23	24	25	26	27
28	29	30				

September
1952

Twinkle. Twinkle little star,
How I wonder what you are,
Up above the world so high,
Like a diamond in the sky.

When the blazing sun is set,
And the grass with dew is wet,
Then you show your little light.
Twinkle, twinkle all the night.

Then, if I were in the dark
I'd thank you for your spark;
I could not see which way to go
If you did not twinkle so.

And when I am sound asleep,
Oft you thru my window peep;
For you never shut your eye
Till the sun is in the sky.

McGuffeys reader
(not written by U.S. Moore)

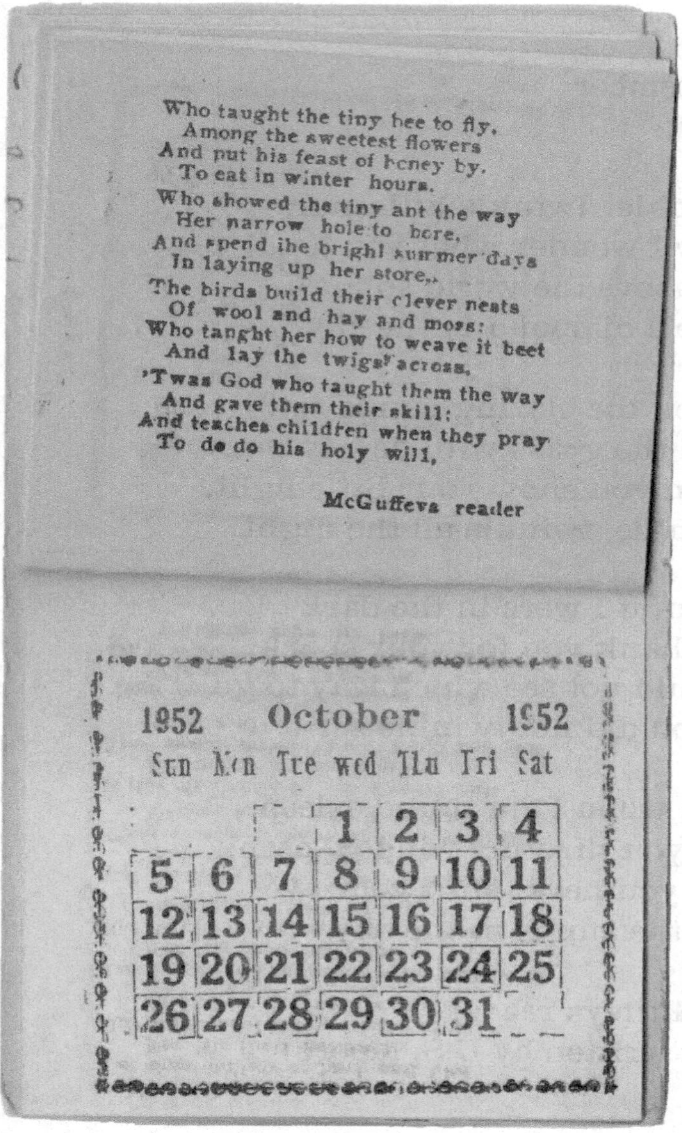

Who taught the tiny bee to fly,
Among the sweetest flowers
And put his feast of honey by,
To eat in winter hours.

Who showed the tiny ant the way
Her narrow hole to bore,
And spend the bright summer days
In laying up her store,.

The birds build their clever nests
Of wool and hay and moss:
Who taught her how to weave it best
And lay the twigs' across,

'Twas God who taught them the way
And gave them their skill:
And teaches children when they pray
To do do his holy will,

McGuffeys reader

1952			October			1952
Sun	Mon	Tue	wed	Thu	Fri	Sat
			1	2	3	4
5	6	7	8	9	10	11
12	13	14	15	16	17	18
19	20	21	22	23	24	25
26	27	28	29	30	31	

October
1952

Who taught the tiny bee to fly,
Among the sweetest flowers
And put his feast of honey by
To eat in winter hours.

Who showed the tiny ant the way
Her narrow hole to bore,
And spend the bright summer days
In laying up her store.

The birds build their clever nests
Of wool and hay and moss;
Who taught her how to weave it beet
And lay the twigs across.

'Twas God who taught them the way
And gave them their skill;
And teaches children when they pray
To do His holy will.

McGuffeys reader
(not written by U.S. Moore)

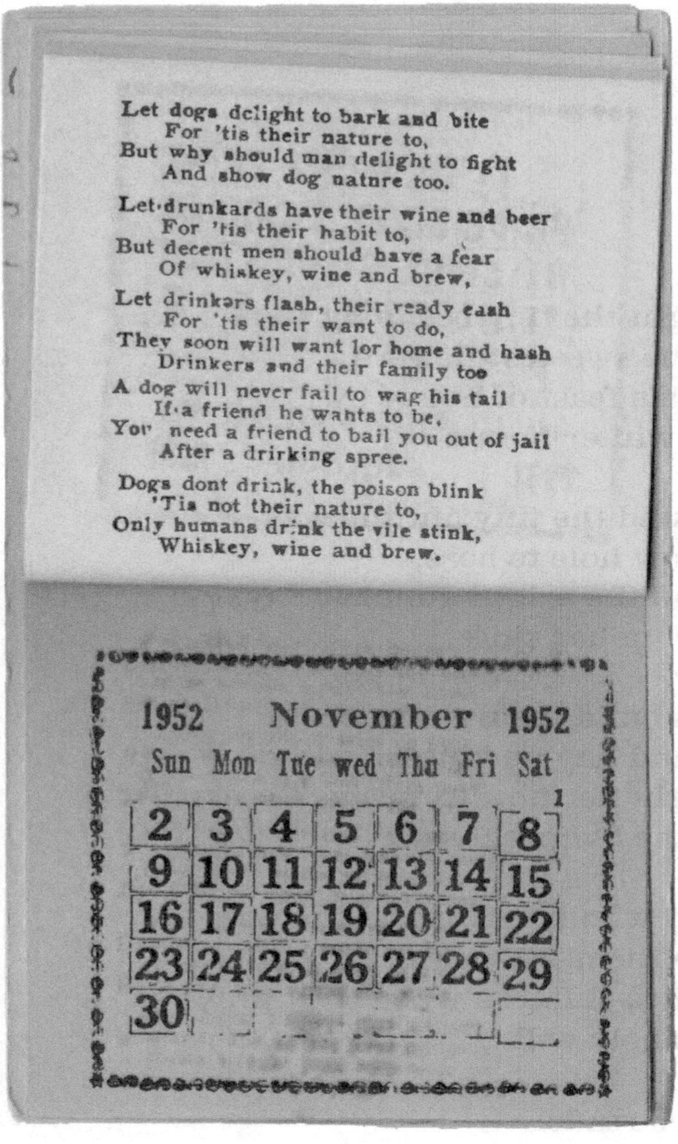
Let dogs delight to bark and bite
For 'tis their nature to,
But why should man delight to fight
And show dog natnre too.
Let drunkards have their wine and beer
For 'tis their habit to,
But decent men should have a fear
Of whiskey, wine and brew,
Let drinkers flash, their ready cash
For 'tis their want to do,
They soon will want lor home and hash
Drinkers and their family too
A dog will never fail to wag his tail
If a friend he wants to be,
You need a friend to bail you out of jail
After a drinking spree.
Dogs dont drink, the poison blink
'Tis not their nature to,
Only humans drink the vile stink,
Whiskey, wine and brew.
1952 November 1952
Sun Mon Tue wed Thu Fri Sat
1
2 3 4 5 6 7 8
9 10 11 12 13 14 15
16 17 18 19 20 21 22
23 24 25 26 27 28 29
30

November
1952

Let dogs delight to bark and bite
For 'tis their nature to,
But why should man delight to fight
And show dog nature too.

Let drunkards have their wine and beer
For 'tis their habit to,
But decent men should have a fear
Of whiskey, wine and brew.

Let drinkers flash their ready cash
For 'tis their want to do.
They soon will want for home and hash
Drinkers and their family too.

A dog will never fail to wag his tail
If a friend he wants to be.
You need a friend to bail you out of jail
After a drinking spree.

Dogs don't drink, the poison blink
'Tis not their nature to.
Only humans drink the vile stink,
Whiskey, wine and brew.

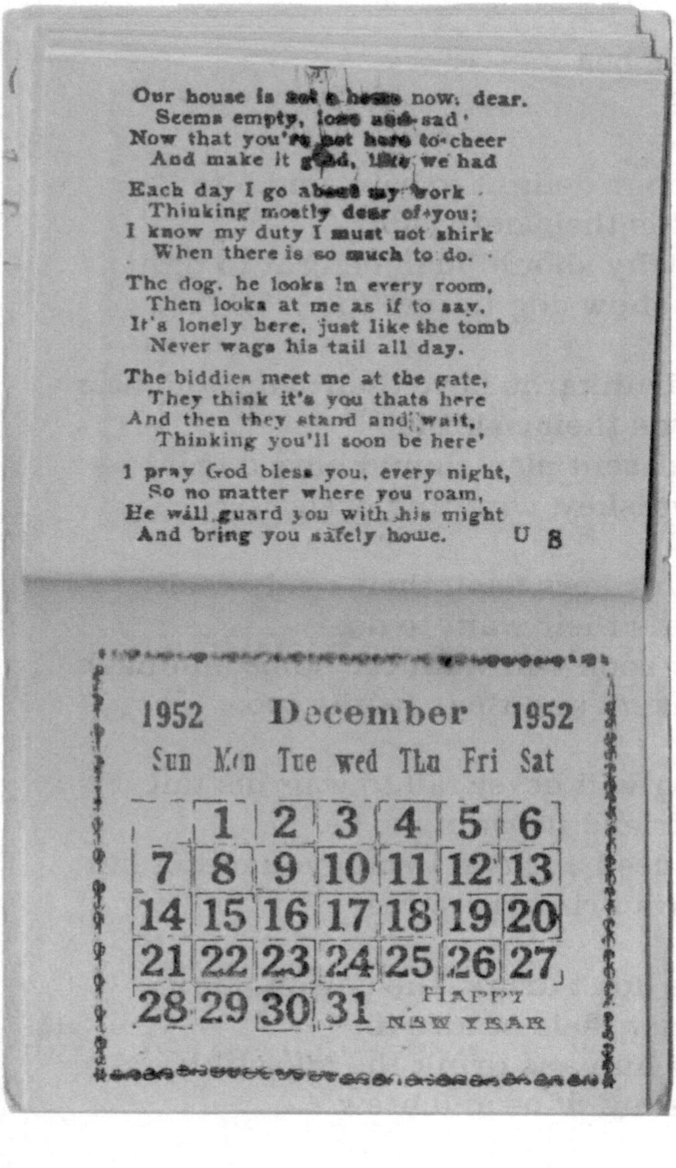

Our house is not a home now, dear.
Seems empty, lone and sad
Now that you're not here to cheer
And make it glad, like we had

Each day I go about my work
Thinking mostly dear of you;
I know my duty I must not shirk
When there is so much to do.

The dog, he looks in every room,
Then looks at me as if to say,
It's lonely here, just like the tomb
Never wags his tail all day.

The biddies meet me at the gate,
They think it's you thats here
And then they stand and wait,
Thinking you'll soon be here'

I pray God bless you, every night,
So no matter where you roam,
He will guard you with his might
And bring you safely home. U S

1952 December 1952

Sun	Mon	Tue	wed	Thu	Fri	Sat
	1	2	3	4	5	6
7	8	9	10	11	12	13
14	15	16	17	18	19	20
21	22	23	24	25	26	27
28	29	30	31			

HAPPY NEW YEAR

December
1952

Our house is not a home now, dear.
Seems empty, loss and sad
Now that you're not here to cheer
And make it glad, like we had.

Each day I go about my work
Thinking mostly dear of you;
I know my duty I must not shirk
When there is so much to do.

The dog, he looks in every room,
Then looks at me as if to say,
It's lonely here, just like the tomb
Never wags his tail all day.

The biddies meet me at the gate,
They think it's you that's here
And then they stand and wait,
Thinking you'll soon be here.

I pray God bless you, every night,
So no matter where you roam
He will guard you with his might
And bring you safely home.

I love the cheerful summer time,
With its birds and flowers,
Its shining garments green,
Its cool refreshing showers.

I love to hear the pretty birds,
That sing among the trees;
I love the gentle flowing stream
I love tha evening breeze.

To think of Him who made,
These pleasant things for me,
Who gave me life and health,
And eyes that I might see.

McGuffeys reader

We harp about the good old time
We could buy a dozen eggs for a dime.
And a dime is what you got when sold
One dollar a day, was the pay in gold.

Ten loaves of breaa for work one day;
Now fifty loave for eight hours pay.
And now, for one hour we get more pay
Than we got then for a whol long day.

One days work, or one bushel of corn
Will buy more goo's, in any form.
And save more money, to lay in store.
Thau we could in good old times before.

High cost of living lies in drinking beer
Whiskey, wine and brew; harm you,
In dance halls, shows and taverns,
In many kinds of gambling too.

In idle time, rideing round in cars,
In wasted spending of your dough.
And wasted hours, playing cards
That's the high cost of living now. U S

1952

I love the cheerful summer time
With its birds and flowers,
Its shining garments green,
Its cool refreshing showers.

I love to hear the pretty birds
That sing among the trees;
I love the gentle flowing stream
I love the evening breeze.

To think of Him who made
These pleasant things for me,
Who gave me life and health
And eyes that I might see.

McGuffey reader
(not written by U.S. Moore)

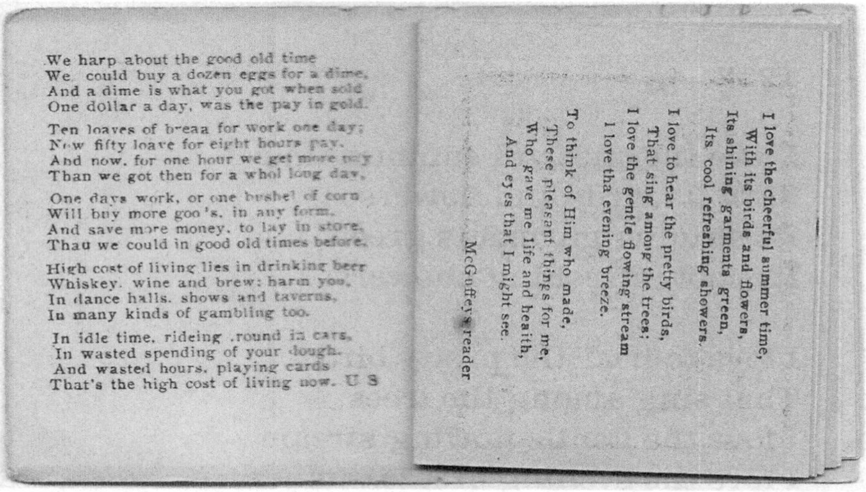
We harp about the good old time
We could buy a dozen eggs for a dime,
And a dime is what you got when sold
One dollar a day, was the pay in gold.

Ten loaves of breaa for work one day;
Now fifty loave for eight hours pay.
And now, for one hour we get more pay
Than we got then for a whol long day.

One days work, or one bushel of corn
Will buy more goo's, in any form.
And save more money, to lay in store,
Thau we could in good old times before.

High cost of living lies in drinking beer
Whiskey, wine and brew; harm you.
In dance halls, shows and taverns,
In many kinds of gambling too.

In idle time, rideing round in cars,
In wasted spending of your dough.
And wasted hours, playing cards
That's the high cost of living now. U S

I love the cheerful summer time,
With its birds and flowers,
Its shining garments green,
Its cool refreshing showers.

I love to hear the pretty birds,
That sing among the trees;
I love the gentle flowing stream
I love tha evening breeze.

To think of Him who made,
These pleasant things for me,
Who gave me life and health,
And eyes that I might see.

McGuffeys reader

We harp about the good old time
We could buy a dozen eggs for a dime,
And a dime is what you got when sold
One dollar a day, was the pay in gold.

Ten loaves of bread for work one day;
Now fifty loaves for eight hours pay.
And now, for one hour we get more pay
Than we got then for a whole long day.

One days work, or one bushel of corn
Will buy more goods in any form.
And save money, to lay in store,
Than we could in good old times before.

High cost of living lies in drinking beer
Whiskey, wine and brew; harm you,
In dance halls, shows and taverns,
In many kinds of gambling too.

In idle time, riding around in cars,
In wasted spending of your dough
And wasted hours, playing cards.
That's the high cost of living now.

A stamp was used to create the ornate designs shown here.

1953

U.S. & Anna Moore

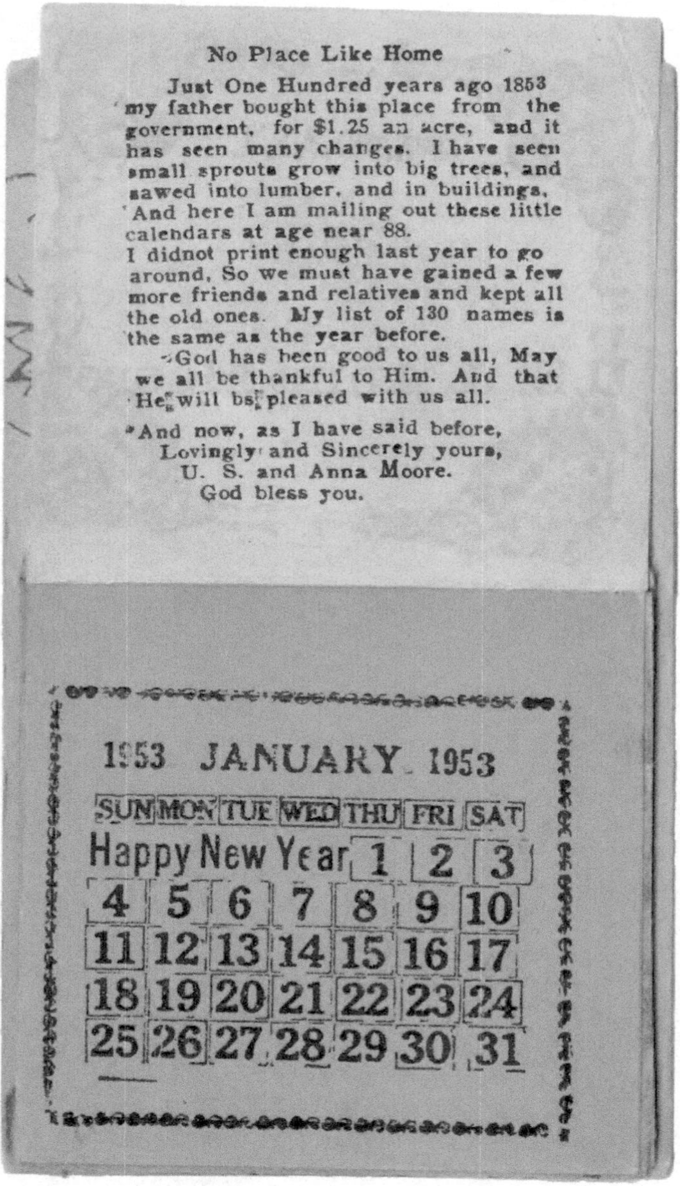

No Place Like Home

Just One Hundred years ago 1853 my father bought this place from the government, for $1.25 an acre, and it has seen many changes. I have seen small sprouts grow into big trees, and sawed into lumber, and in buildings, And here I am mailing out these little calendars at age near 88.
I didnot print enough last year to go around, So we must have gained a few more friends and relatives and kept all the old ones. My list of 130 names is the same as the year before.

God has been good to us all, May we all be thankful to Him. And that He will be pleased with us all.

And now, as I have said before,
Lovingly and Sincerely yours,
U. S. and Anna Moore.
God bless you.

1953 JANUARY 1953

SUN	MON	TUE	WED	THU	FRI	SAT
Happy New Year				1	2	3
4	5	6	7	8	9	10
11	12	13	14	15	16	17
18	19	20	21	22	23	24
25	26	27	28	29	30	31

January
1953

No Place Like Home

Just One Hundred years ago 1853 my father bought this place from the government, for $1.25 an acre, and it has seen many changes. I have seen small sprouts grow into big trees, and sawed into lumber, and in buildings.

And here I am mailing out these little calendars at age near 88.

I did not print enough last year to go around, so we must have gained a few more friends and relatives and kept all the old ones. My list of 130 names is the same as the year before.

God has been good to us all. May we all be thankful to Him. And that He will be pleased with us all.

And now, as I have said before,
Lovingly and Sincerely yours,
U.S. and Anna Moore.
God bless you.

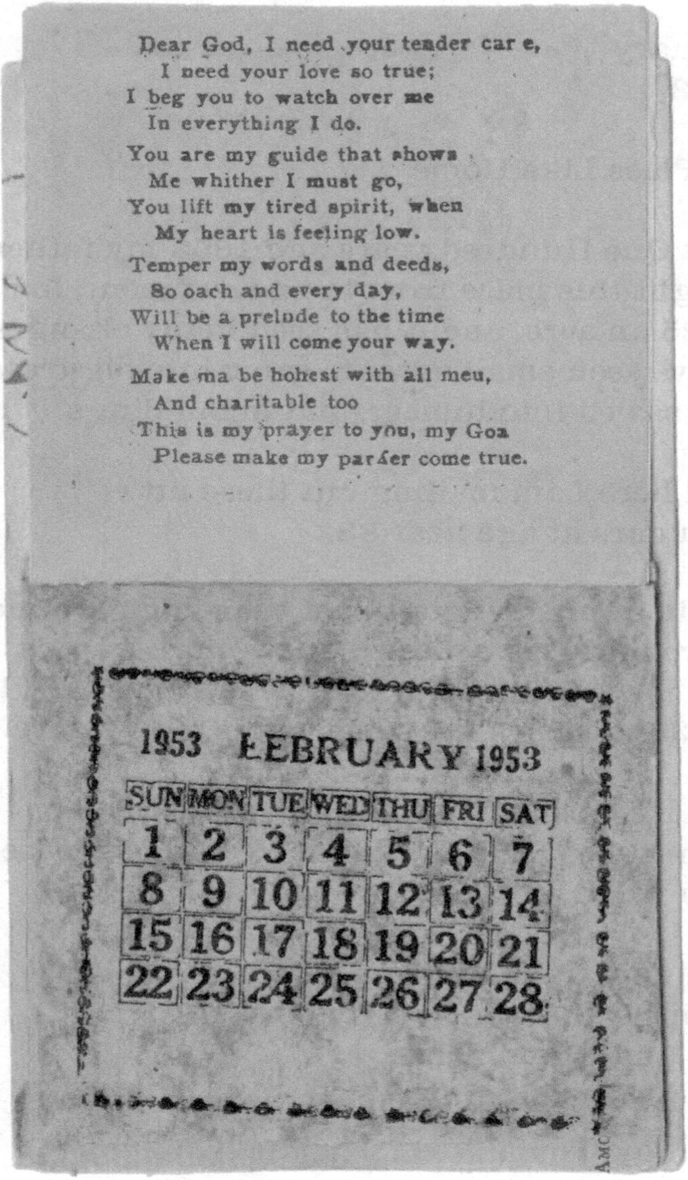
Dear God, I need your teader car e,
I need your love so true;
I beg you to watch over me
In everything I do.
You are my guide that shows
Me whither I must go,
You lift my tired spirit, when
My heart is feeling low.
Temper my words and deeds,
So oach and every day,
Will be a prelnde to the time
When I will come your way.
Make ma be hohest with all meu,
And charitable too
This is my prayer to you, my Goa
Please make my parker come true.
1953 FEBRUARY 1953
SUN MON TUE WED THU FRI SAT
1 2 3 4 5 6 7
8 9 10 11 12 13 14
15 16 17 18 19 20 21
22 23 24 25 26 27 28

February
1953

Dear God, I need your tender care,
I need your love so true;
I beg you to watch over me
In everything I do.

You are my guide that shows
Me whither I must go,
You lift my tired spirit, when
My heart is feeling low.

Temper my words and deeds,
So each and every day
Will be a prelude to the time
When I will come your way.

Make me be honest with all men,
And charitable too.
This is my prayer to you, my God
Please make my prayer come true.

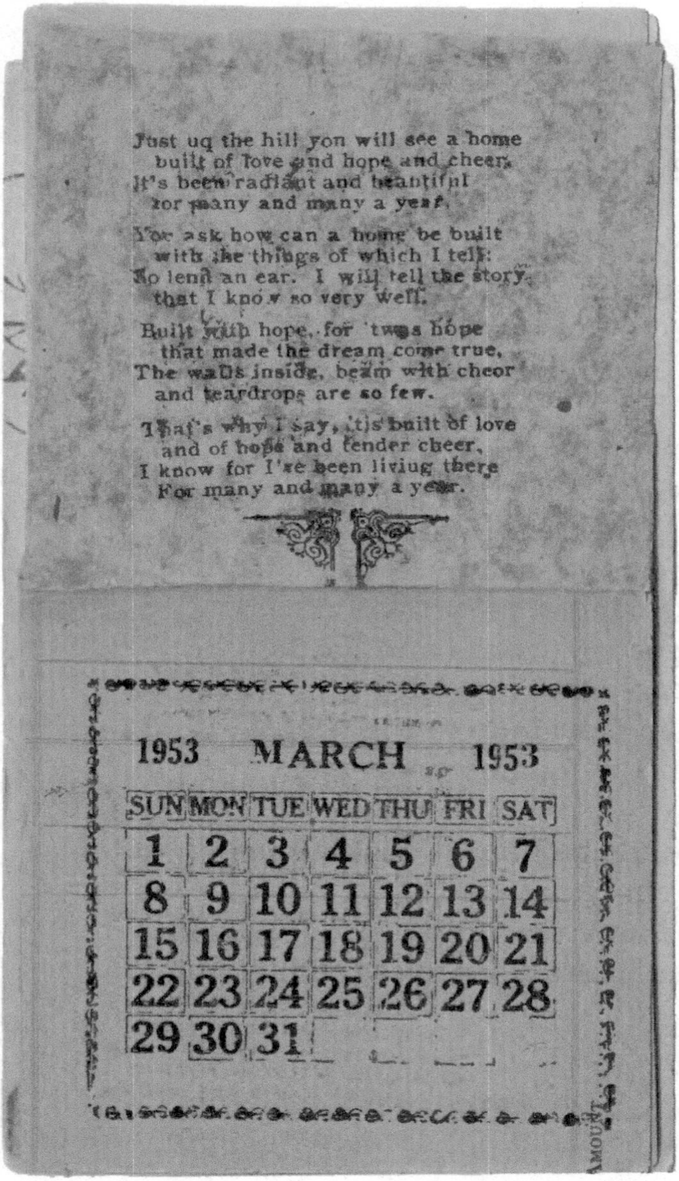

Just uq the hill yon will see a home
built of love and hope and cheer.
It's been radiant and beautiful
for many and many a year.

You ask how can a home be built
with the things of which I tell:
So lend an ear. I will tell the story
that I know so very well.

Built with hope, for 'twas hope
that made the dream come true,
The walls inside, beam with cheor
and teardrops are so few.

That's why I say, 'tis built of love
and of hope and tender cheer,
I know for I've been liviug there
For many and many a year.

1953 MARCH 1953

SUN	MON	TUE	WED	THU	FRI	SAT
1	2	3	4	5	6	7
8	9	10	11	12	13	14
15	16	17	18	19	20	21
22	23	24	25	26	27	28
29	30	31				

March
1953

Just up the hill you will see a home
built of love and hope and cheer.
It's been radiant and beautiful
for many and many a year.

You ask how can a home be built
with the things of which I tell;
So lend an ear. I will tell the story
that I know so very well.

Built with hope, for 'twas hope
that made the dream come true,
The walls inside beam with cheer
and teardrops are so few.

That's why I say, 'tis built of love
and of hope and tender cheer.
I know for I've been living there
for many and many a year.

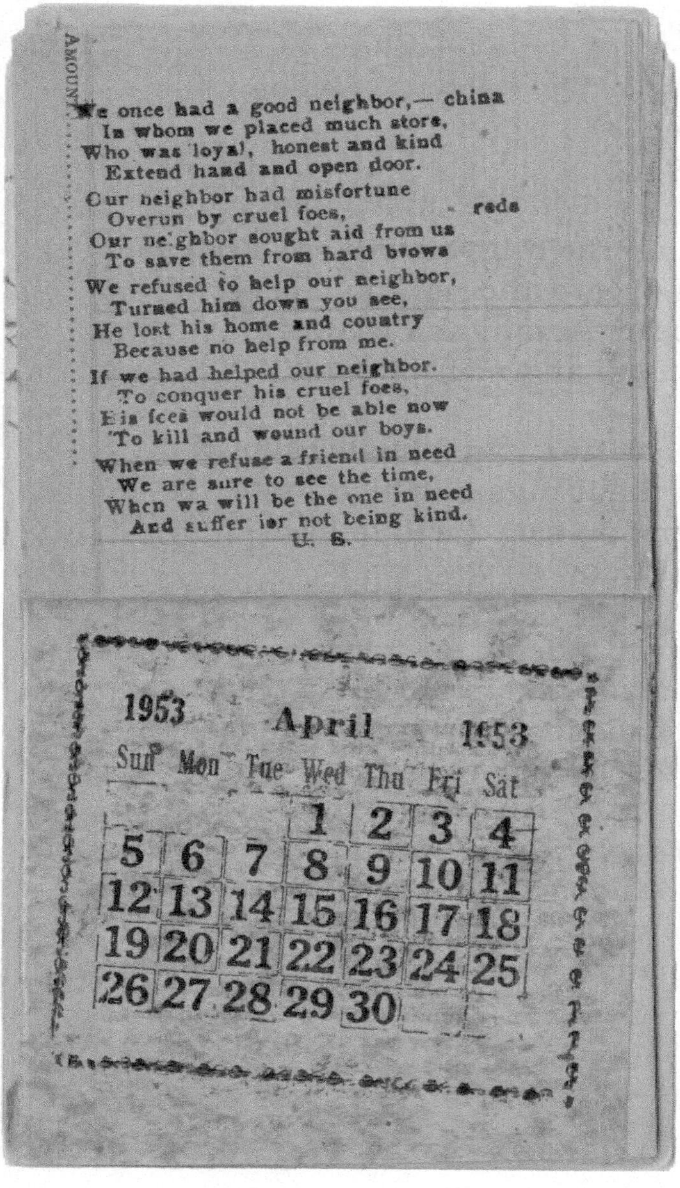

AMOUNT

We once had a good neighbor,— china
In whom we placed much store,
Who was loyal, honest and kind
Extend hand and open door.

Our neighbor had misfortune
Overun by cruel foes, reds
Our neighbor sought aid from us
To save them from hard brows

We refused to help our neighbor,
Turned him down you see,
He lost his home and country
Because no help from me.

If we had helped our neighbor.
To conquer his cruel foes,
His foes would not be able now
To kill and wound our boys.

When we refuse a friend in need
We are sure to see the time,
When wa will be the one in need
And suffer ior not being kind.

U. S.

1953 April 1953

Sun	Mon	Tue	Wed	Thu	Fri	Sat
			1	2	3	4
5	6	7	8	9	10	11
12	13	14	15	16	17	18
19	20	21	22	23	24	25
26	27	28	29	30		

April
1953

We once had a good neighbor - China
In whom we placed much store.
Who was loyal, honest and kind
Extend hand and open door.

Our neighbor had misfortune
Overrun by cruel foes - reds
Our neighbor sought aid from us
To save them from hard brows.

We refused to help our neighbor;
Turned him down you see.
He lost his home and country
Because no help from me.

If we had helped our neighbor
To conquer his cruel foes,
His foes would not be able now
To kill and wound our boys.

When we refuse a friend in need
We are sure to see the time
When we will be the one in need
And suffer for not being kind.

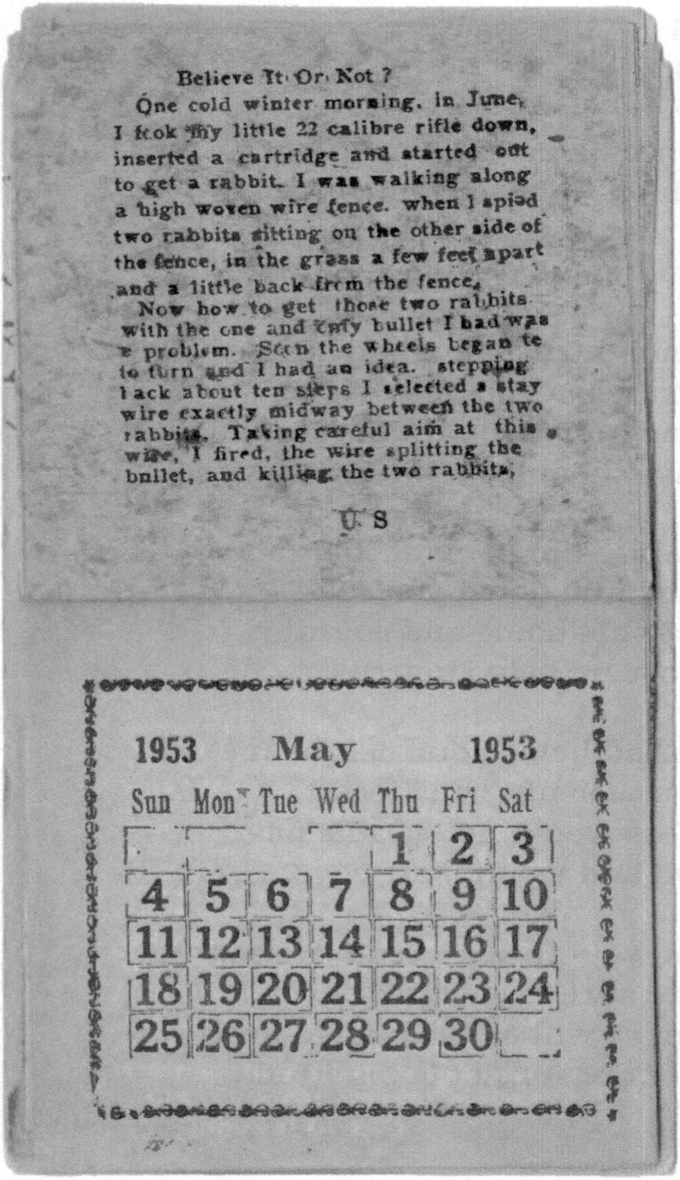

Believe It Or Not ?

One cold winter morning, in June, I took my little 22 calibre rifle down, inserted a cartridge and started out to get a rabbit. I was walking along a high woven wire fence. when I spied two rabbits sitting on the other side of the fence, in the grass a few feet apart and a little back from the fence.

Now how to get those two rabbits with the one and only bullet I had was a problem. Soon the wheels began to turn and I had an idea. stepping back about ten steps I selected a stay wire exactly midway between the two rabbits. Taking careful aim at this wire, I fired, the wire splitting the bullet, and killing the two rabbits,

U S

1953 May 1953

Sun	Mon	Tue	Wed	Thu	Fri	Sat
				1	2	3
4	5	6	7	8	9	10
11	12	13	14	15	16	17
18	19	20	21	22	23	24
25	26	27	28	29	30	

May
1953

Believe It Or Not?

One cold winter morning, in June, I took my little 22 caliber rifle down, inserted a cartridge and started out to get a rabbit. I was walking along a high woven wire fence when I spied two rabbits sitting on the other side of the fence, in the grass a few feet apart and a little back from the fence.

Now how to get those two rabbit with the one and only bullet I had was a problem. Soon the wheels began to turn and I had an idea. Stepping back about ten steps I selected a stay wire exactly midway between the two rabbits. Taking careful aim at this wire, I fired, the wire splitting the bullet, and killing the two rabbits.

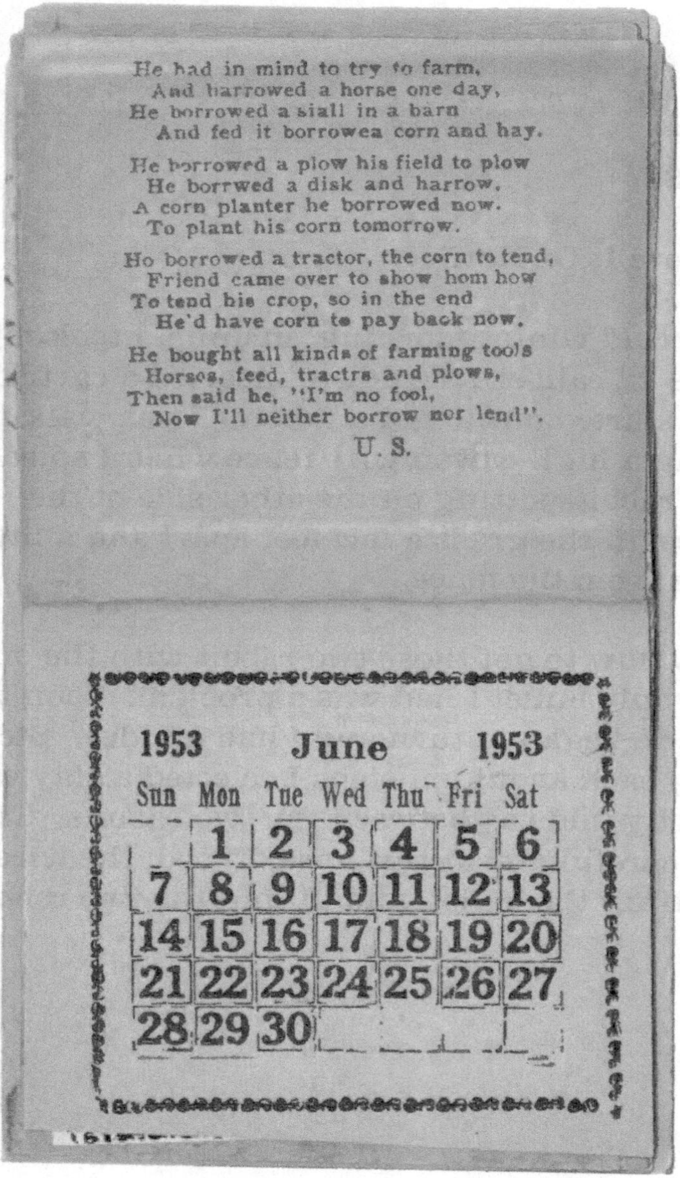

He had in mind to try to farm,
And harrowed a horse one day,
He borrowed a siall in a barn
And fed it borrowea corn and hay.

He borrowed a plow his field to plow
He borrwed a disk and harrow,
A corn planter he borrowed now.
To plant his corn tomorrow.

Ho borrowed a tractor, the corn to tend,
Friend came over to show hom how
To tend his crop, so in the end
He'd have corn to pay back now.

He bought all kinds of farming tools
Horses, feed, tractrs and plows,
Then said he, "I'm no fool,
Now I'll neither borrow nor lend".

U. S.

1953 June 1953

Sun	Mon	Tue	Wed	Thu	Fri	Sat
	1	2	3	4	5	6
7	8	9	10	11	12	13
14	15	16	17	18	19	20
21	22	23	24	25	26	27
28	29	30				

June
1953

He had in mind to try to farm,
And borrowed a horse one day.
He borrowed a stall in a barn
And fed it borrowed corn and hay.

He borrowed a plow his field to plow.
He borrowed a disk and harrow.
A corn planter he borrowed now
To plant his corn tomorrow.

He borrowed a tractor, the corn to tend.
Friend came over to show him how
To tend his crop, so in the end
He'd have corn to pay back now.

He bought all kinds of farming tools,
Horses, feed, tractors and plows.
Then said he, "I'm no fool,
Now I'll neither borrow nor lend."

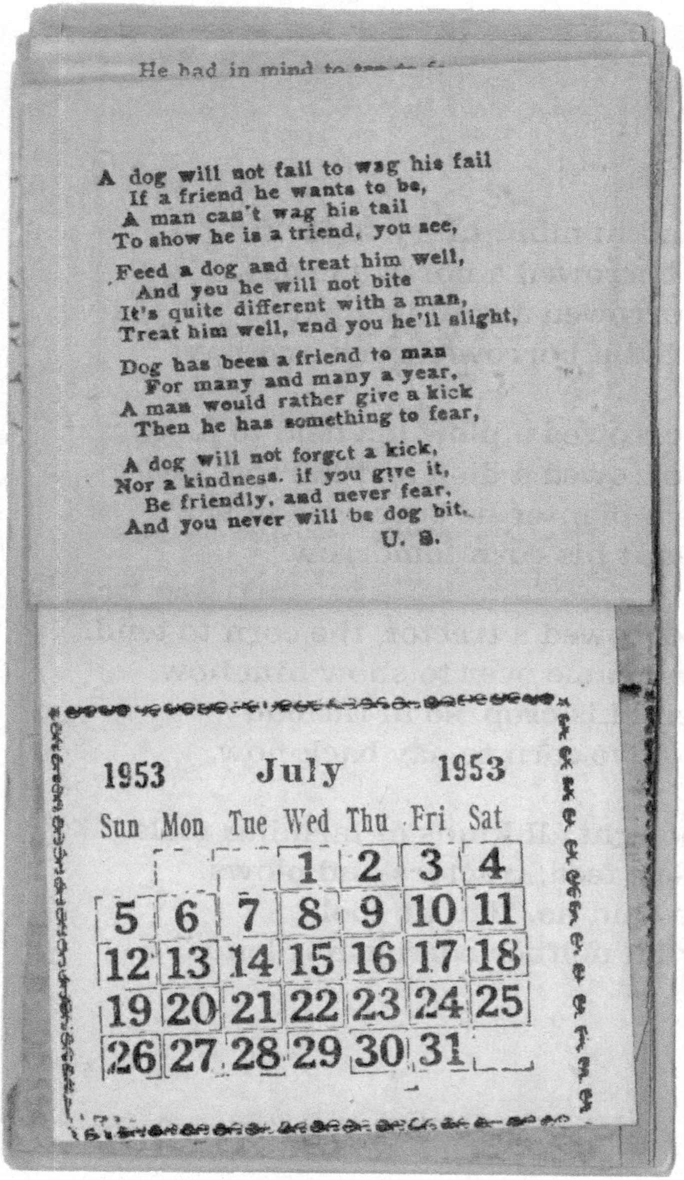
He had in mind to
A dog will not fail to wag his fail
If a friend he wants to be,
A man can't wag his tail
To show he is a triend, you see,
Feed a dog and treat him well,
And you he will not bite
It's quite different with a man,
Treat him well, and you he'll slight,
Dog has been a friend to man
For many and many a year,
A man would rather give a kick
Then he has something to fear,
A dog will not forget a kick,
Nor a kindness. if you give it,
Be friendly, and never fear,
And you never will be dog bit.
U. S.
1953 July 1953
Sun Mon Tue Wed Thu Fri Sat
1 2 3 4
5 6 7 8 9 10 11
12 13 14 15 16 17 18
19 20 21 22 23 24 25
26 27 28 29 30 31

July
1953

A dog will not fail to wag his tail
If a friend he wants to be.
A man can't wag his tail
To show he is a friend, you see.

Feed a dog and treat him well,
And you he will not bite.
It's quite different with a man
For many and many a year,
A man would rather give a kick
Then he has something to fear.

A dog will not forget a kick,
Nor a kindness, if you give it.
Be friendly, and never fear,
And you never will be dog bit.

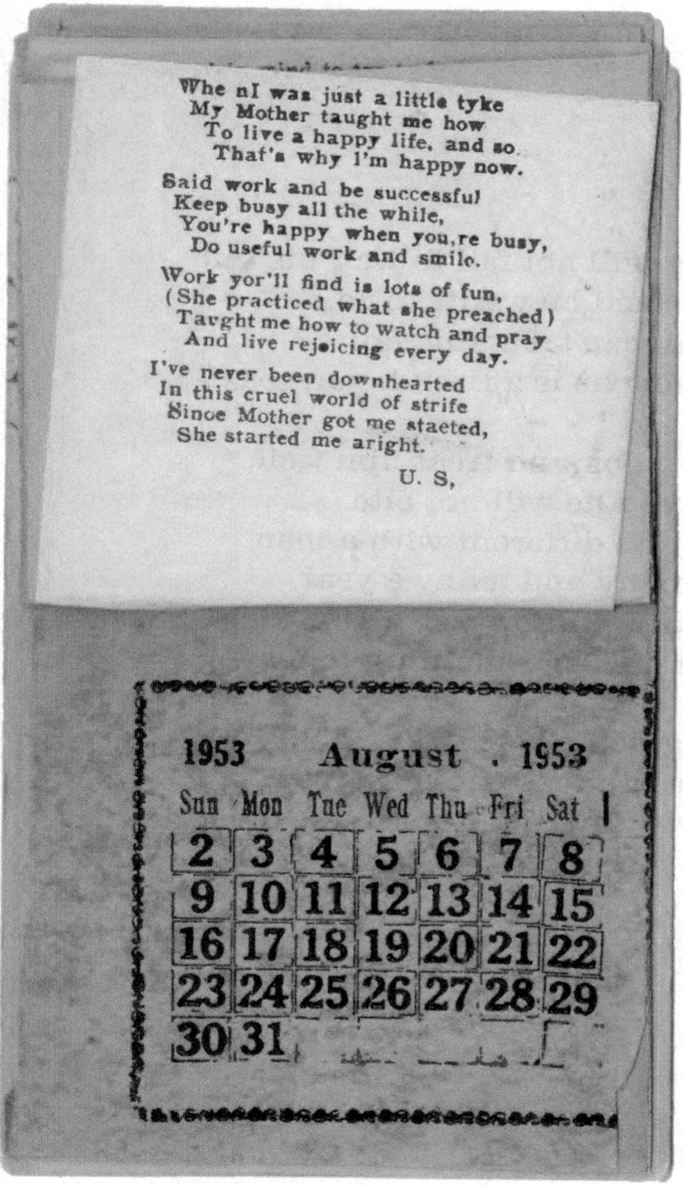
Whe nI was just a little tyke
My Mother taught me how
To live a happy life, and so.
That's why I'm happy now.
Said work and be successful
Keep busy all the while,
You're happy when you,re busy,
Do useful work and smile.
Work yor'll find is lots of fun,
(She practiced what she preached)
Tavght me how to watch and pray
And live rejoicing every day.
I've never been downhearted
In this cruel world of strife
Since Mother got me staeted,
She started me aright.
U. S,
1953 August . 1953
Sun Mon Tue Wed Thu Fri Sat
2 3 4 5 6 7 8
9 10 11 12 13 14 15
16 17 18 19 20 21 22
23 24 25 26 27 28 29
30 31

August
1953

When I was just a little tyke
My Mother taught me how
To live a happy life, and so
That's why I'm happy now.

Said work and be successful,
Keep busy all the while,
You're happy when you're busy.
Do useful work and smile.

Work you'll find is lots of fun
(She practiced what she preached).
Taught me how to watch and pray
And live rejoicing every day.

I've never been downhearted
In this cruel world of strife
Since Mother got me started.
She started me aright.

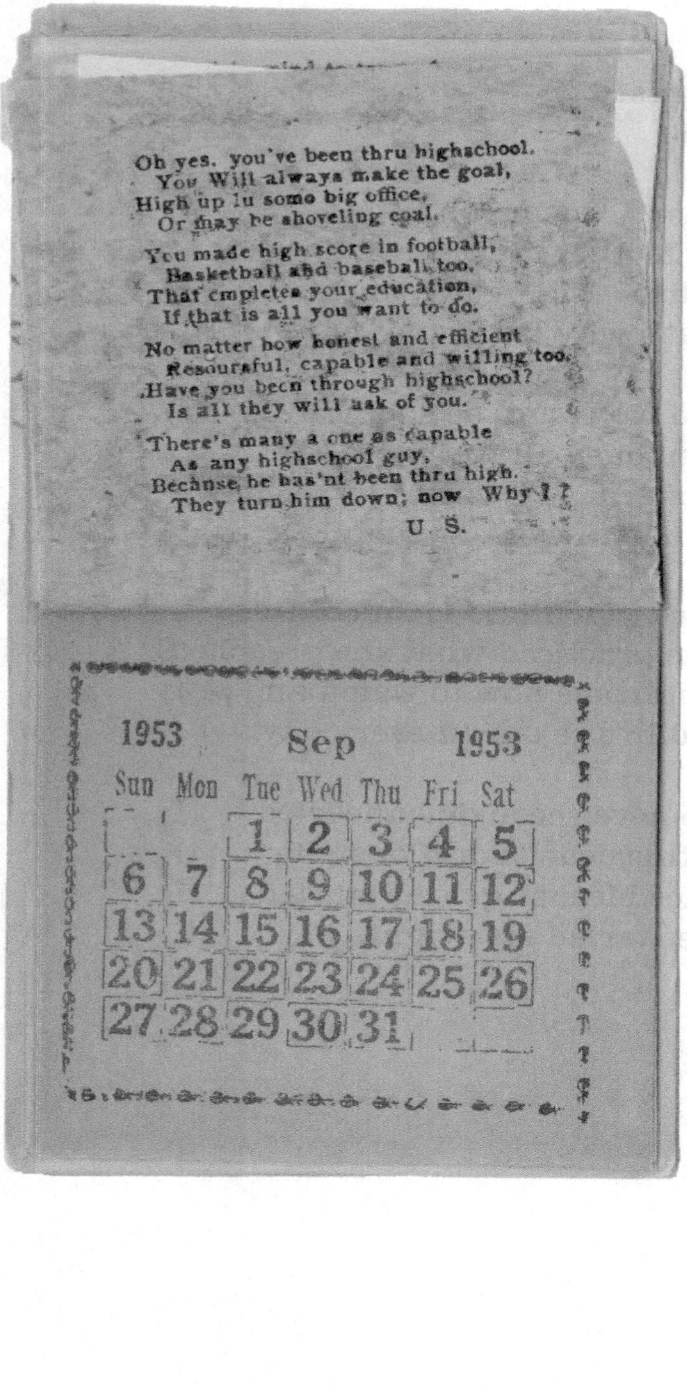

Oh yes, you've been thru highschool.
You Will alwaya make the goal,
High up lu some big office,
Or may be shoveling coal.

You made high score in football,
Basketball and baseball too.
That completes your education,
If that is all you want to do.

No matter how honest and efficient
Resoursful, capable and willing too.
Have you been through highschool?
Is all they will ask of you.

There's many a one as capable
As any highschool guy,
Because he has'nt been thru high.
They turn him down; now Why ? ?

U. S.

1953			Sep			1953
Sun	Mon	Tue	Wed	Thu	Fri	Sat
		1	2	3	4	5
6	7	8	9	10	11	12
13	14	15	16	17	18	19
20	21	22	23	24	25	26
27	28	29	30	31		

September
1953

O yes, you've been thru high school.
You will always make the goal.
High up in some big office,
Or maybe shoveling coal.

You made high score in football,
Basketball and baseball, too.
That completes your education,
If that is all you want to do.

No matter how honest and efficient
Resourceful, capable and willing, too,
Have you been through high school?
Is all they will ask of you.

There's many a one as capable
As any high school guy
Because he hasn't been thru high
They turn him down; now Why?

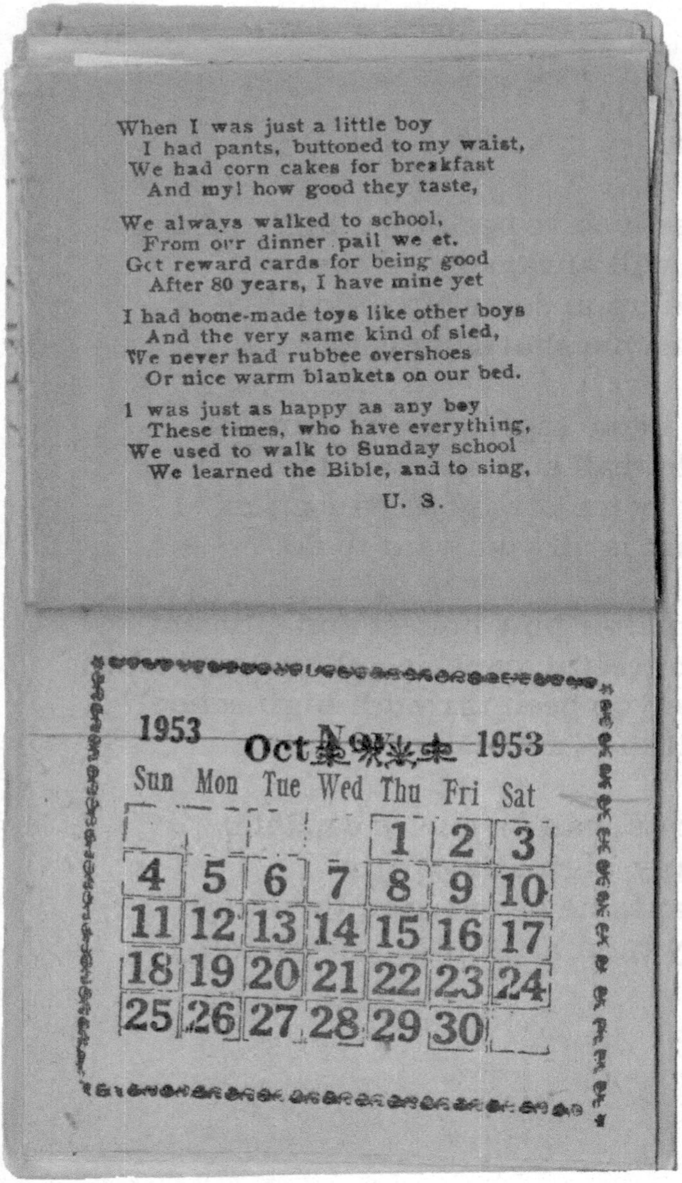

When I was just a little boy
I had pants, buttoned to my waist,
We had corn cakes for breakfast
And my! how good they taste,

We always walked to school,
From our dinner pail we et.
Got reward cards for being good
After 80 years, I have mine yet

I had home-made toys like other boys
And the very same kind of sled,
We never had rubbee overshoes
Or nice warm blankets on our bed.

I was just as happy as any boy
These times, who have everything,
We used to walk to Sunday school
We learned the Bible, and to sing,

U. S.

1953 Oct Nov 1953

Sun	Mon	Tue	Wed	Thu	Fri	Sat
				1	2	3
4	5	6	7	8	9	10
11	12	13	14	15	16	17
18	19	20	21	22	23	24
25	26	27	28	29	30	

October
1953

When I was just a little boy
I had pants, buttoned to my waist.
We had corn cakes for breakfast
And my! how good they taste.

We always walked to school,
From our dinner pail we et,
Got reward cards for being good.
After 80 years, I have mine yet.

I had home-made toys like other boys
And this very same kind of sled.
We never had rubber overshoes
Or nice warm blankets on our bed.

I was just as happy as any boy.
These times, who have everything,
We used to walk to Sunday school.
We learned the Bible, and to sing.

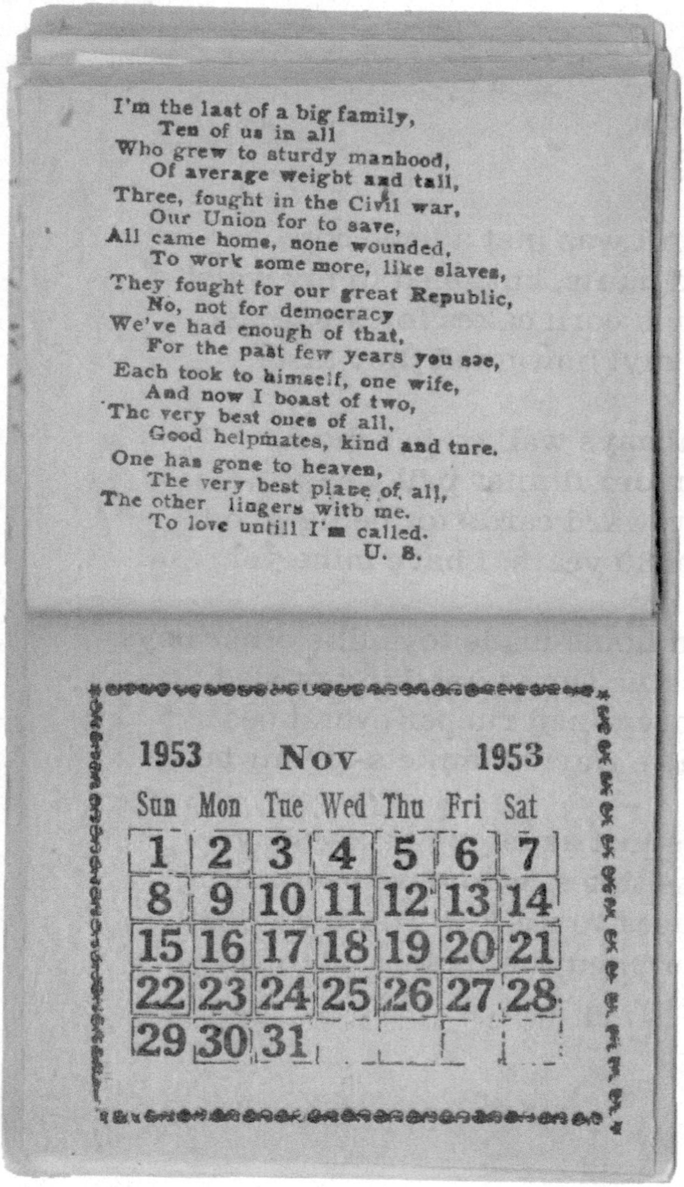
I'm the last of a big family,
Ten of us in all
Who grew to sturdy manhood,
Of average weight and tall,
Three, fought in the Civil war,
Our Union for to save,
All came home, none wounded,
To work some more, like slaves,
They fought for our great Republic,
No, not for democracy
We've had enough of that,
For the past few years you see,
Each took to himself, one wife,
And now I boast of two,
Thc very best ones of all,
Good helpmates, kind and ture.
One has gone to heaven,
The very best plane of all,
The other lingers witb me.
To love untill I'm called.
U. S.
1953 Nov 1953
Sun Mon Tue Wed Thu Fri Sat
1 2 3 4 5 6 7
8 9 10 11 12 13 14
15 16 17 18 19 20 21
22 23 24 25 26 27 28
29 30 31

November
1953

I'm the last of a big family,
Ten of us in all,
Who grew to sturdy manhood,
Of average weight and tall.

Three, fought in the Civil war,
Our Union for to save.
All came home, none wounded,
to work some more, like slaves.

They fought for our great Republic,
No, not for democracy.
We've had enough of that,
For the past few years you see.

Each took to himself, one wife,
And now I boast of two,
The very best ones of all,
Good helpmates, kind and true.

One has gone to heaven,
The very best place of all.
The other lingers with me
To love until I'm called.

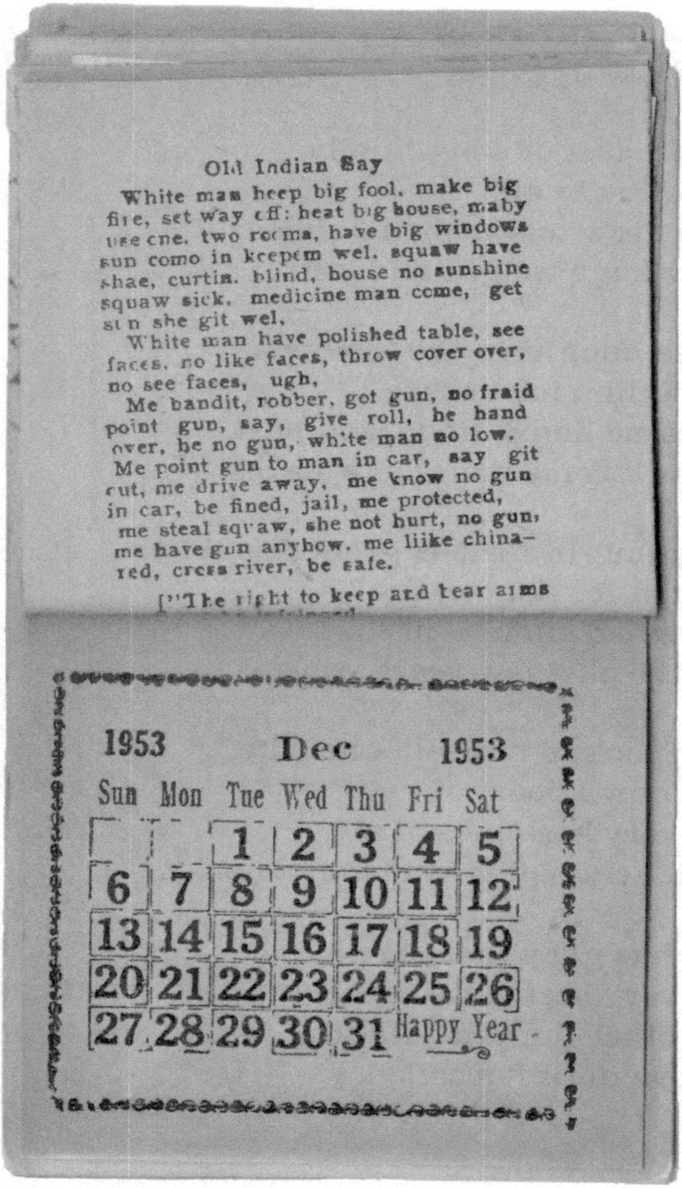
Old Indian Say
White man heep big fool, make big fire, set way off: heat big house, maby use one, two rooms, have big windows sun como in keepem wel, squaw have shae, curtin, blind, house no sunshine squaw sick, medicine man come, get sun she git wel,
White man have polished table, see faces, no like faces, throw cover over, no see faces, ugh,
Me bandit, robber, got gun, no fraid point gun, say, give roll, he hand over, he no gun, white man no low.
Me point gun to man in car, say git out, me drive away, me know no gun in car, be fined, jail, me protected, me steal sqaw, she not hurt, no gun, me have gun anyhow, me liike china-red, cross river, be safe.
["The right to keep and bear arms
1953 Dec 1953
Sun Mon Tue Wed Thu Fri Sat
1 2 3 4 5
6 7 8 9 10 11 12
13 14 15 16 17 18 19
20 21 22 23 24 25 26
27 28 29 30 31 Happy Year

December
1953

Old Indian Say

White man heep big fool, make big fire, set way off: heat big house, maybe use one, two rooms, have big windows. Sun come in keep em well. Squaw have shade, curtain, blind. House no sunshine. Squaw sick, medicine man come, get sun she get well.

White man have polished table, see faces, no like faces, throw cover over, no see faces. Ugh.

Me bandit, robber, got gun, no afraid, point gun, say, give roll, he hand over, he no gun, white man no low.

Me point gun to man in car, say get out, me drive away, me know no gun in car, be fined, jail, me protected.

Me steal squaw, she not hurt, no gun. Me have gun anyhow, me like china - red, cross river, be safe.

[The right to keep and bear arms should not be infringed.]

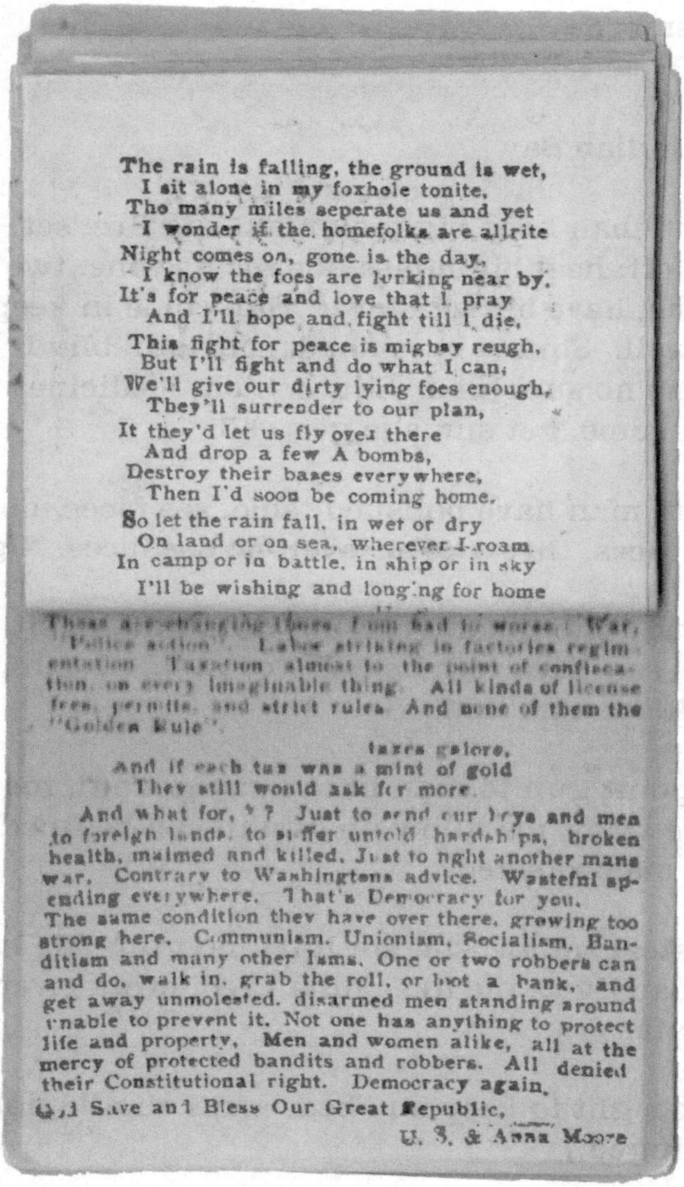

The rain is falling, the ground is wet,
I sit alone in my foxhole tonite,
Tho many miles seperate us and yet
I wonder if the homefolks are allrite
Night comes on, gone is the day,
I know the foes are lurking near by,
It's for peace and love that I pray
And I'll hope and fight till I die,
This fight for peace is mighty rough,
But I'll fight and do what I can;
We'll give our dirty lying foes enough,
They'll surrender to our plan,
It they'd let us fly over there
And drop a few A bombs,
Destroy their bases everywhere,
Then I'd soon be coming home.
So let the rain fall, in wet or dry
On land or on sea, wherever I roam
In camp or in battle, in ship or in sky
I'll be wishing and longing for home

These are changing times, from bad to worse. War, "Police action". Labor striking in factories regimentation. Taxation almost to the point of confiscation on every imaginable thing. All kinds of license fees, permits, and strict rules. And none of them the "Golden Rule".

taxes galore,
And if each tax was a mint of gold
They still would ask for more.

And what for, ?? Just to send our boys and men to foreign lands, to suffer untold hardships, broken health, maimed and killed. Just to fight another mans war, Contrary to Washingtons advice. Wasteful spending everywhere. That's Democracy for you.
The same condition they have over there, growing too strong here. Communism. Unionism. Socialism. Banditism and many other Isms. One or two robbers can and do, walk in, grab the roll, or loot a bank, and get away unmolested, disarmed men standing around unable to prevent it. Not one has anything to protect life and property. Men and women alike, all at the mercy of protected bandits and robbers. All denied their Constitutional right. Democracy again.
God Save and Bless Our Great Republic,

U. S. & Anna Moore

1953

The rain is falling, the ground is wet.
I sit alone in my foxhole tonight,
The many miles separate us and yet
I wonder if the homefolks are alright.

Night comes on, gone is the day.
I know the foes are lurking nearby.
It's for peace and love that I pray.
And I'll hope and fight till I die.

This fight for peace is mighty rough,
But I'll fight and do what I can.
We'll give our dirty lying foes enough.
They'll surrender to our plan.

If they'd let us fly over there
And drop a few A bombs,
Destroy their bases everywhere,
Then I'd soon be coming home.

So let the rain fall. In wet or dry,
On land or on sea, wherever I roam
In camp or in battle, in ship or in sky
I'd be wishing and longing for home.

Another calendar another year passed by. These are changing times. from bad to worse. War, "Police action". Labor striking in factories regimentation. Taxation almost to the point of confiscation. on every imaginable thing. All kinds of license fees, permits, and strict rules. And none of them the "Golden Rule".

taxes galore,
And if each tax was a mint of gold
They still would ask for more.

And what for, ? ? Just to send our boys and men to foreign lands. to suffer untold hardships, broken health, maimed and killed. Just to fight another mans war. Contrary to Washingtons advice. Wastefnl spending everywhere. That's Democracy for you.
The same condition they have over there. growing too strong here. Communism. Unionism. Socialism. Banditism and many other Isms. One or two robbers can and do, walk in. grab the roll. or loot a bank, and get away unmolested. disarmed men standing around unable to prevent it. Not one has anything to protect life and property. Men and women alike, all at the mercy of protected bandits and robbers. All denied their Constitutional right. Democracy again.

God Save and Bless Our Great Republic,

U. S. & Anna Moore

Another calendar, another year passed by. These are changing times. From bad to worse. War, "Police action". Labor striking in factories regimentation. Taxation almost to the point of confiscation, on every imaginable thing. All kinds of license fees, permits, and strict rules. And none of them the "Golden Rule".

Taxes galore
And if each tax was a mint of gold
They still would ask for more.

And what for?? Just to send our boys and men to foreign lands, to suffer untold hardships, broken health, maimed and killed. Just to fight another mans war. Contrary to Washington's advice. Wasteful spending everywhere. That's Democracy for you.

The same condition they have over there, growing too strong here. Communism. Unionism. Socialism. Banditism and many other Isms. One or two robbers can and do walk in, grab the roll, or loot a bank, and get away unmolested, disarmed men standing around unable to prevent it. Not one has anything to protect life and property. Men and women alike, all at the mercy of protected bandits and robbers. All denied their Constitutional right. Democracy again.

God Save and Bless Our Great Republic,
U. S. & Anna Moore

This is an actual photo of U.S. Moore's mother, Harriett.

1956

Mother

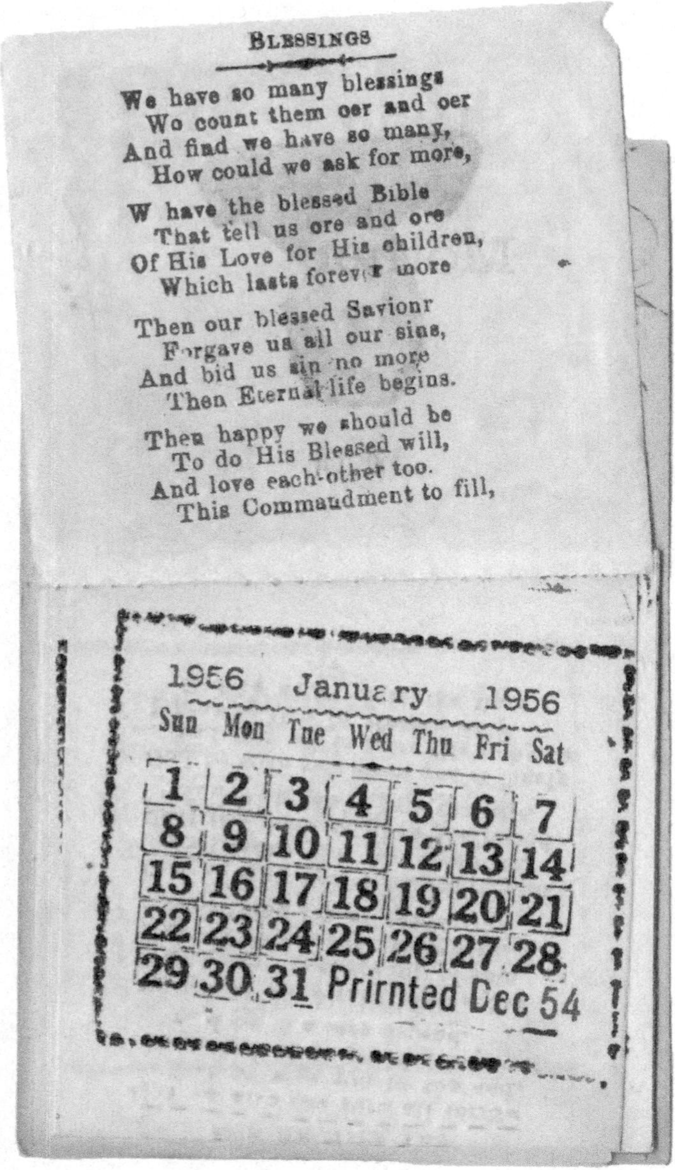

BLESSINGS

We have so many blessings
Wo count them oer and oer
And find we have so many,
How could we ask for more,

W have the blessed Bible
That tell us ore and ore
Of His Love for His children,
Which lasts forever more

Then our blessed Savionr
Forgave us all our sins,
And bid us sin no more
Then Eternal life begins.

Then happy we should be
To do His Blessed will,
And love each other too.
This Commaudment to fill,

1956 January 1956

Sun	Mon	Tue	Wed	Thu	Fri	Sat
1	2	3	4	5	6	7
8	9	10	11	12	13	14
15	16	17	18	19	20	21
22	23	24	25	26	27	28
29	30	31				

Prirnted Dec 54

January
1956

Blessings

We have so many blessings
We count them over and over
And find we have so many,
How could we ask for more.

We have the blessed Bible
That tell us over and over
Of His Love for His children
Which lasts forever more.

Then our blessed Savior
Forgave us all our sins
And bid us sin no more.
Then Eternal life begins.

Then happy we should be
To do His Blessed will,
And love each other too.
This commandment to fill.

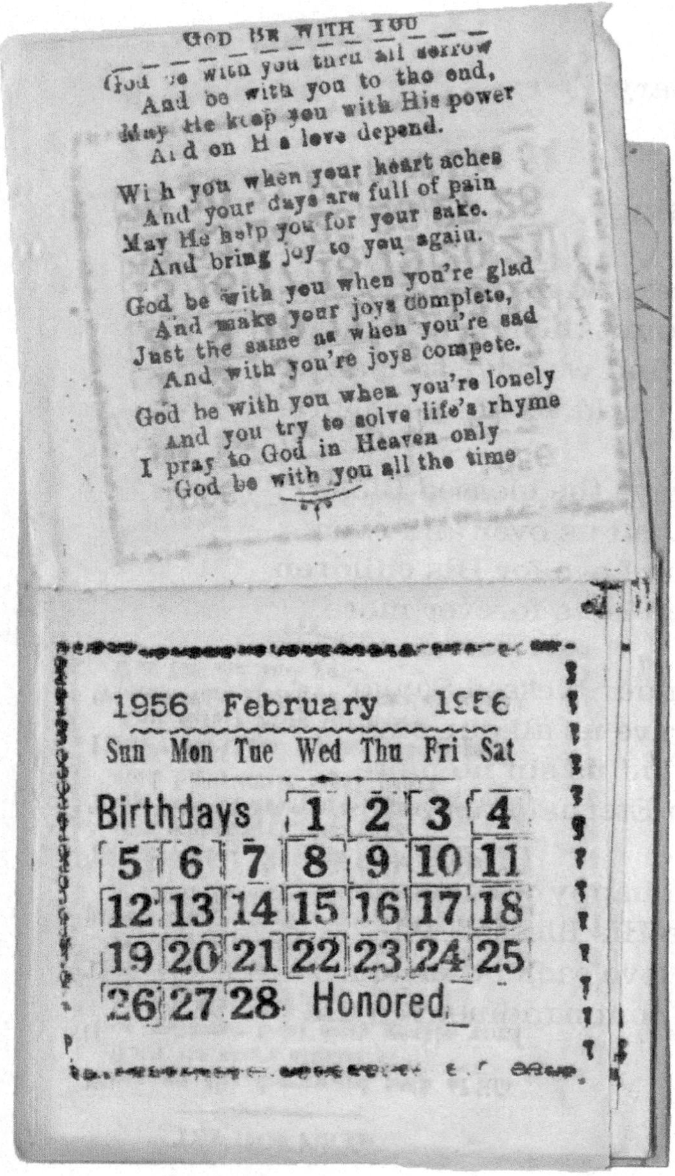
GOD BE WITH YOU
And be with you to the end,
May He keep you with His power
And on His love depend.
With you when your heart aches
And your days are full of pain
May He help you for your sake.
And bring joy to you again.
God be with you when you're glad
And make your joys complete,
Just the same as when you're sad
And with you're joys compete.
God be with you when you're lonely
And you try to solve life's rhyme
I pray to God in Heaven only
God be with you all the time
1956 February 1956
Sun Mon Tue Wed Thu Fri Sat
Birthdays 1 2 3 4
5 6 7 8 9 10 11
12 13 14 15 16 17 18
19 20 21 22 23 24 25
26 27 28 Honored

February
1956

God Be With You

God be with you thru all sorrow
And be with you to the end.
May He keep you with His power
And on His love depend.

Wish you when your heart aches
And your days are full of pain
May He help you for your sake,
And bring joy to you again.

God be with you when you're glad
And make your joys complete.
Just the same as when you're sad
And with your joys compete.

God be with you when you're lonely
And you try to solve life's rhyme.
I pray to God in Heaven only
God be with you all the time.

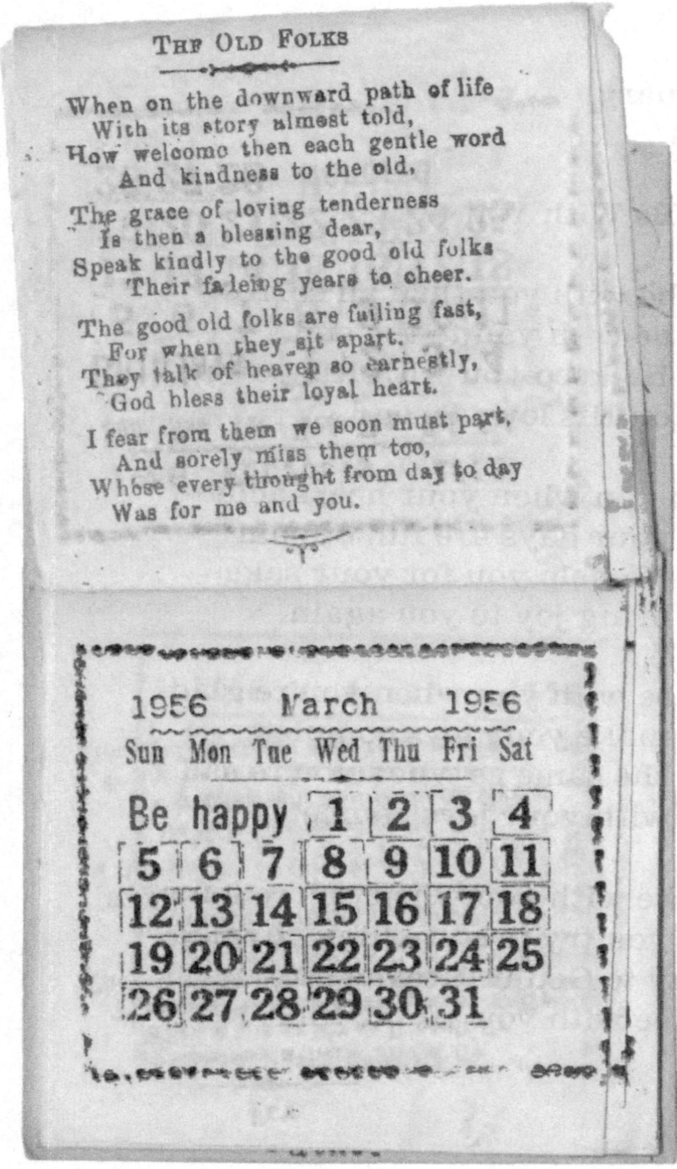
THE OLD FOLKS
When on the downward path of life
With its story almost told,
How welcome then each gentle word
And kindness to the old.
The grace of loving tenderness
Is then a blessing dear,
Speak kindly to the good old folks
Their faleing years to cheer.
The good old folks are failing fast,
For when they sit apart.
They talk of heaven so earnestly,
God bless their loyal heart.
I fear from them we soon must part,
And sorely miss them too,
Whose every throught from day to day
Was for me and you.
1956 March 1956
Sun Mon Tue Wed Thu Fri Sat
Be happy 1 2 3 4
5 6 7 8 9 10 11
12 13 14 15 16 17 18
19 20 21 22 23 24 25
26 27 28 29 30 31

March
1956

The Old Folks

When on the downward path of life
With its story almost told,
How welcome then each gentle word
And kindness to the old.

The grace of loving tenderness
Is then a blessing dear.
Speak kindly to the good old folks
Their fading years to cheer.

The good old folks are failing fast,
For when they sit apart
They talk of heaven so earnestly.
God bless their loyal heart.

I fear from them we soon must part
And sorely miss them too.
Whose every thought from day to day
Was for me and you.

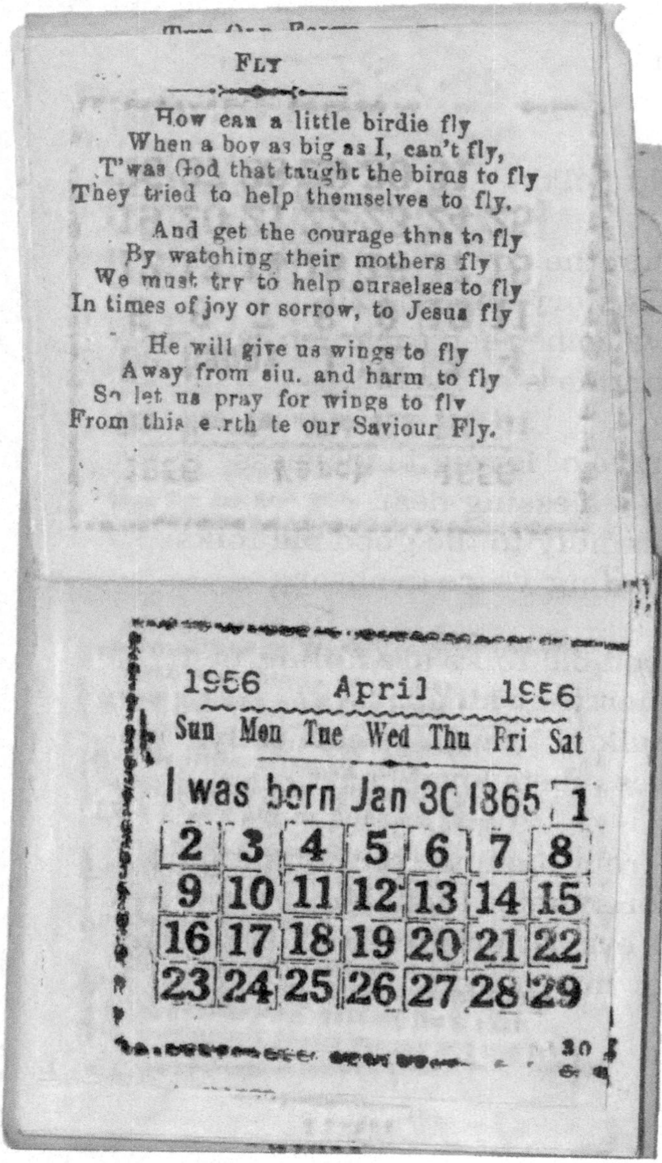

FLY

How can a little birdie fly
When a boy as big as I, can't fly,
T'was God that taught the birds to fly
They tried to help themselves to fly.

And get the courage thus to fly
By watching their mothers fly
We must try to help ourselses to fly
In times of joy or sorrow, to Jesus fly

He will give us wings to fly
Away from sin. and harm to fly
So let us pray for wings to fly
From this earth te our Saviour Fly.

1956 April 1956

Sun	Mon	Tue	Wed	Thu	Fri	Sat
I was born Jan 30 1865						1
2	3	4	5	6	7	8
9	10	11	12	13	14	15
16	17	18	19	20	21	22
23	24	25	26	27	28	29
						30

April
1956

Fly

How can a little birdie fly
When a boy as big as I, can't fly.
'Twas God that taught the birds to fly
They tried to help themselves to fly.

And get the courage thus to fly
By watching their mothers fly.
We must try to help ourselves to fly
In times of joy or sorrow, to Jesus fly.

He will give us wings to fly
Away from sin, and harm to fly.
So let us pray for wings to fly
From this earth to our Savior fly.

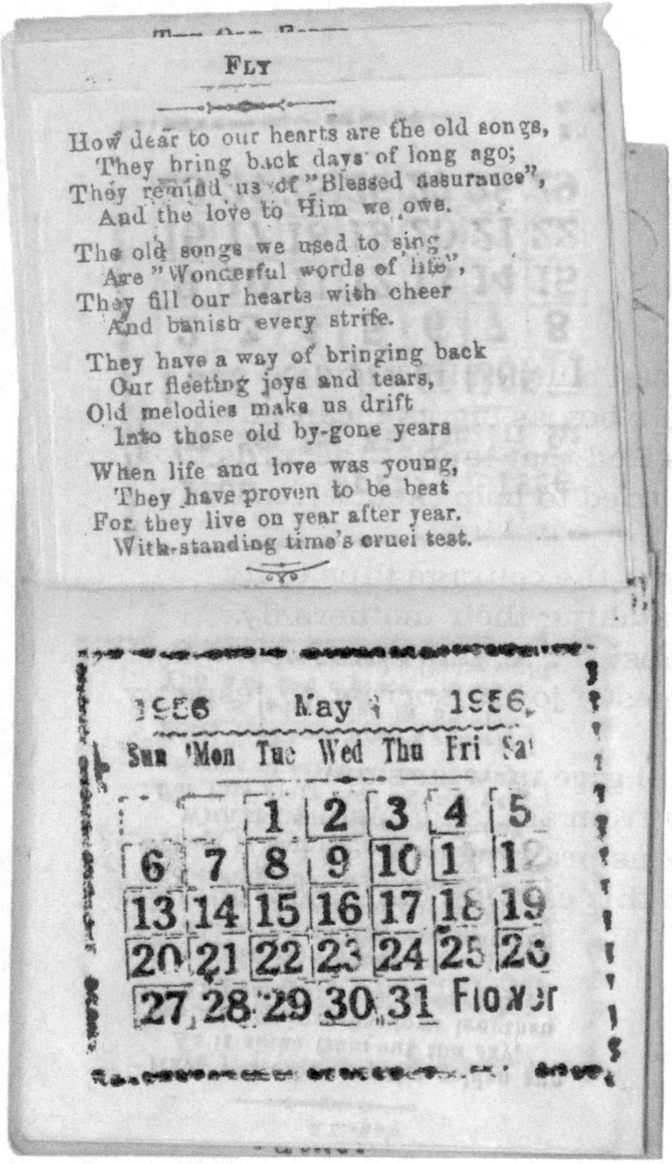

FLY

How dear to our hearts are the old songs,
They bring back days of long ago;
They remind us of "Blessed assurance",
And the love to Him we owe.

The old songs we used to sing
Are "Wonderful words of life",
They fill our hearts with cheer
And banish every strife.

They have a way of bringing back
Our fleeting joys and tears,
Old melodies make us drift
Into those old by-gone years

When life and love was young,
They have proven to be best
For they live on year after year.
With-standing time's cruel test.

1956 May 1956

Sun	Mon	Tue	Wed	Thu	Fri	Sat
		1	2	3	4	5
6	7	8	9	10	11	12
13	14	15	16	17	18	19
20	21	22	23	24	25	26
27	28	29	30	31	Flower	

May
1956

How dear to our hearts are the old songs.
They bring back days of long ago.
They remind us of “Blessed assurance”
And the love to Him we owe.

The old songs we used to sing
Are “Wonderful words of life”.
They fill our hearts with cheer
And banish every strife.

They have a way of bringing back
Our fleeting joys and tears.
Old melodies make us drift
Into those old by-gone years

When life and love was young.
They have proven to be best
For they live on year after year,
Withstanding time’s cruel test.

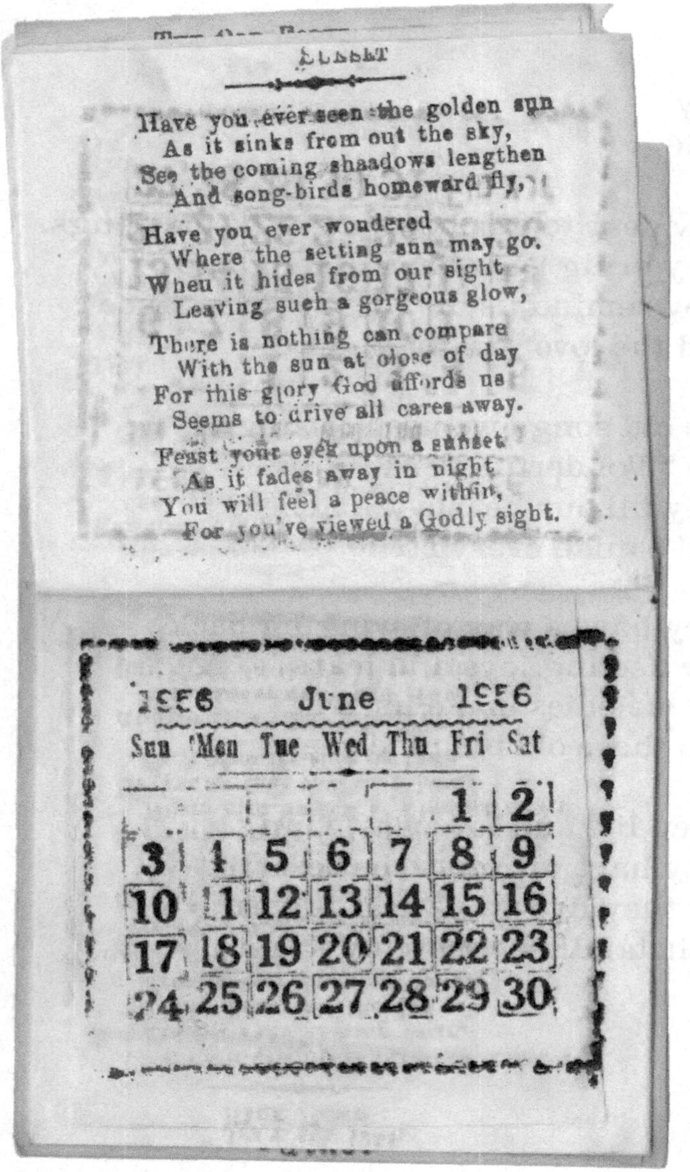

SUNSET

Have you ever seen the golden sun
As it sinks from out the sky,
See the coming shaadows lengthen
And song-birds homeward fly,

Have you ever wondered
Where the setting sun may go.
When it hides from our sight
Leaving such a gorgeous glow,

There is nothing can compare
With the sun at close of day
For this glory God affords us
Seems to drive all cares away.

Feast your eyes upon a sunset
As it fades away in night
You will feel a peace within,
For you've viewed a Godly sight.

1956 June 1956

Sun	Mon	Tue	Wed	Thu	Fri	Sat
					1	2
3	4	5	6	7	8	9
10	11	12	13	14	15	16
17	18	19	20	21	22	23
24	25	26	27	28	29	30

June
1956

Have you ever seen the golden sun
As it sinks from out in the sky?
See the coming shadows lengthen
And song birds homeward fly?

Have you ever wondered
Where the setting sun may go
When it hides from our sight,
Leaving such a gorgeous glow?

There is nothing can compare
With the sun at close of day.
For this glory God affords us
Seems to drive all cares away.

Feast your eyes upon a sunset
As it fades away in night.
You will feel a peace within
For you've viewed a Godly sight.

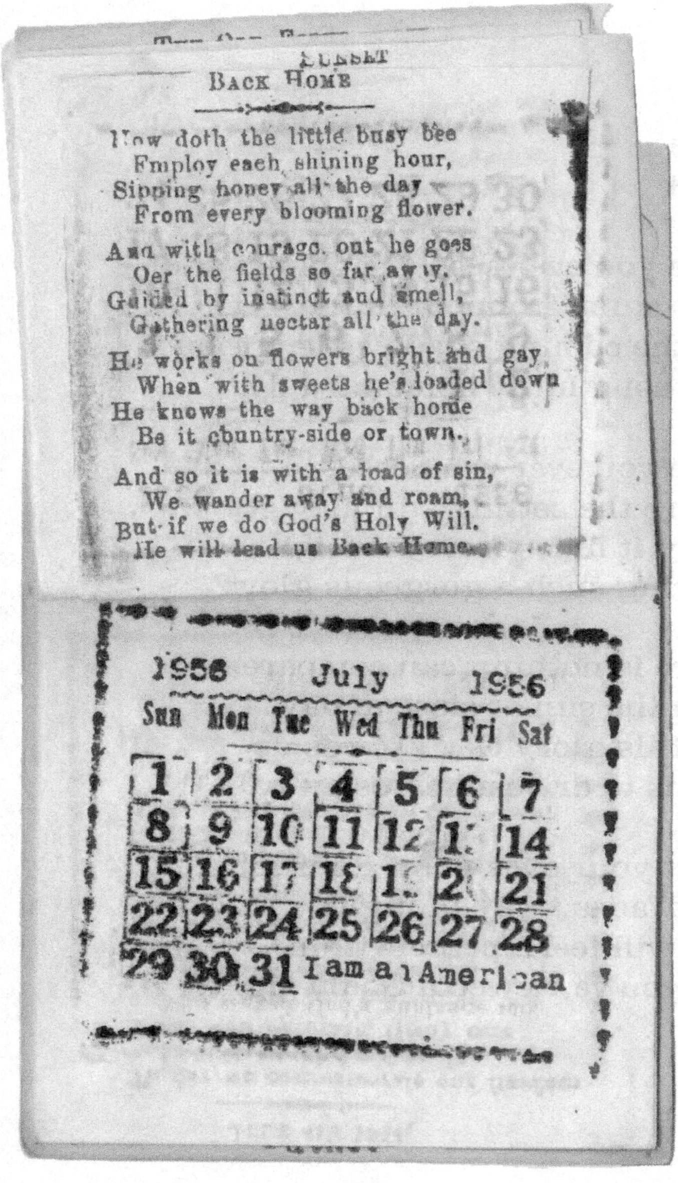

BACK HOME

How doth the little busy bee
Employ each shining hour,
Sipping honey all the day
From every blooming flower.

And with courage out he goes
Oer the fields so far away.
Guided by instinct and smell,
Gathering nectar all the day.

He works on flowers bright and gay
When with sweets he's loaded down
He knows the way back home
Be it country-side or town.

And so it is with a load of sin,
We wander away and roam,
But if we do God's Holy Will.
He will lead us Back Home.

1956 July 1956

Sun	Mon	Tue	Wed	Thu	Fri	Sat
1	2	3	4	5	6	7
8	9	10	11	12	13	14
15	16	17	18	19	20	21
22	23	24	25	26	27	28
29	30	31	I am an American			

July
1956

Back Home

How doth the little busy bee
Employ each shining hour,
Sipping honey all the day
From every blooming flower?

And with courage, out he goes
Over the fields so far away,
Guided by instinct and smell,
Gathering nectar all the day.

He works on flowers bright and gay
When with sweets he's loaded down
He knows the way back home
Be it country-side or town.

And so it is with a load of sin,
We wander away and roam.
But if we do God's Holy Will
He will lead us Back Home.

JULY 4th 1954,
To day we commemorate our freedom
'Twas won by brave, Godly men
Who seeked God's guidance too.
But God was with us all,
He gave us our brave Washington
He would not give up at all
And when hope was almost gone,
He knelt down in the snow
And prayed for courage to fight on,
And won our freedom you know.
He gave us much good advice,
Some is very unheeded
But God is still our refuge,
And is just the One thats needed.
August
Sun Mon Tue Wed Thu Fri Sat
1 2 3 4
5 6 7 8 9 10 11
12 13 14 15 16 17 18
19 20 21 22 23 24 25
26 27 28 29 30 31

August
1956

July 4th
1954

Today we commemorate our freedom
As God would have us do.
T'was won by brave, Godly men
Who seeked God's guidance too.

It seems a hopeless struggle
But God was with us all.
He gives us our brave Washington.
He would not give up at all.

And when hope was almost gone
He knelt down in the snow
And prayed for courage to fight on,
And won our freedom you know.

He gave us much good advice,
Some have gone unheeded.
But God is still our refuge
And is just that One that's needed.

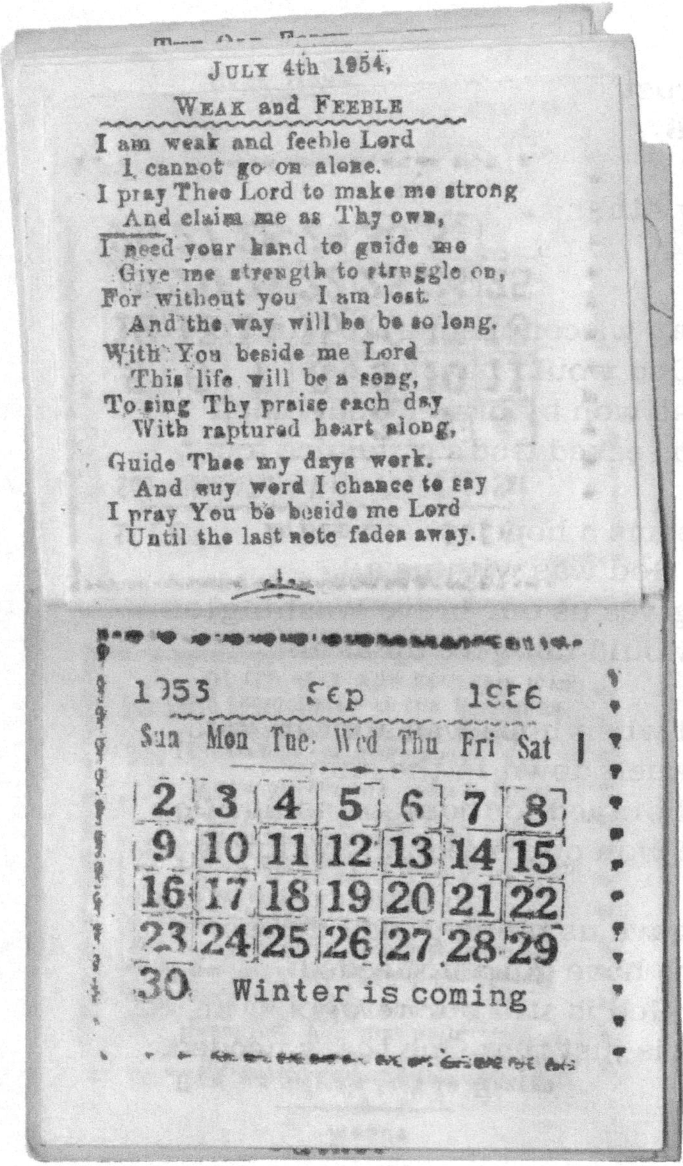
JULY 4th 1954,
WEAK and FEEBLE
I am weak and feeble Lord
I cannot go on alone.
I pray Thee Lord to make me strong
And claim me as Thy own,
I need your hand to guide me
Give me strength to struggle on,
For without you I am lost.
And the way will be be so long.
With You beside me Lord
This life will be a song,
To sing Thy praise each day
With raptured heart along,
Guide Thee my days work.
And any word I chance to say
I pray You be beside me Lord
Until the last note fades away.
1953 Sep 1956
Sun Mon Tue Wed Thu Fri Sat
2 3 4 5 6 7 8
9 10 11 12 13 14 15
16 17 18 19 20 21 22
23 24 25 26 27 28 29
30 Winter is coming

September
1956

Weak and Feeble

I am weak and feeble Lord
I cannot go on alone.
I pray Thee Lord to make me strong
And claim me as Thy own.

I need your hand to guide me
Give me strength to struggle on.
For without you I am lost,
And the way will be so long.

With You beside me Lord
This life will be a song.
To sing Thy praise each day
With raptured heart along,

Guide Thee my days work
And any word I chance to say.
I pray You be beside me Lord
Until the last note fades away.

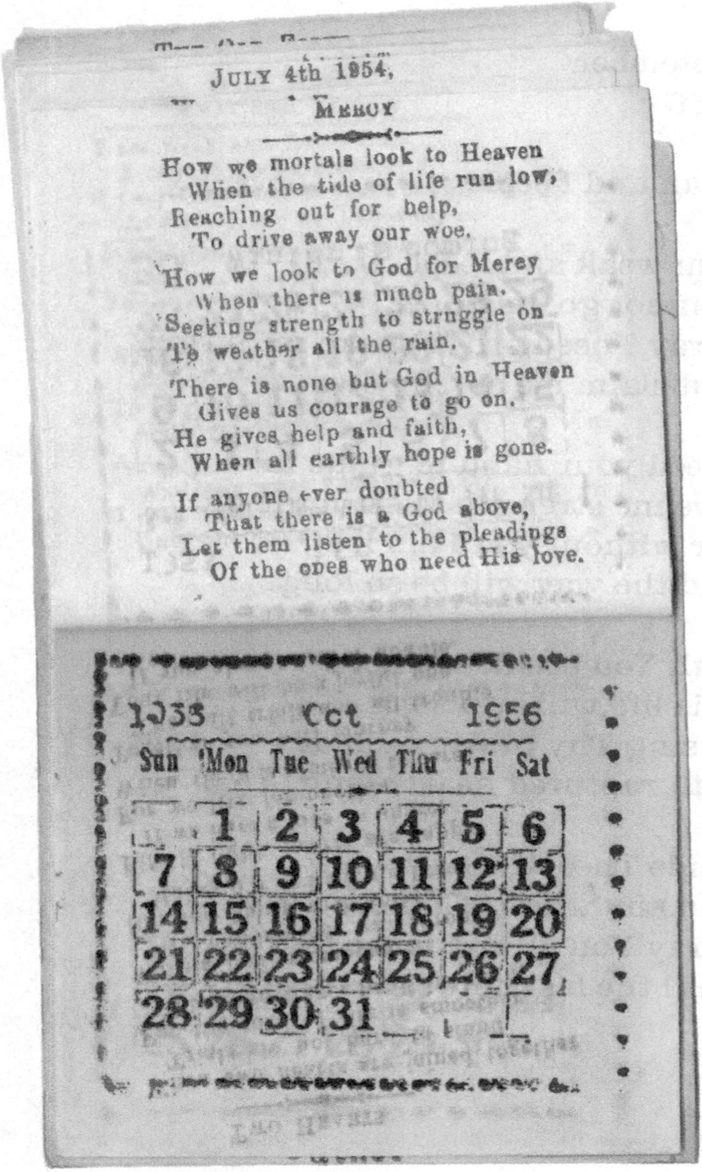
JULY 4th 1954,
MERCY
How we mortals look to Heaven
When the tide of life run low,
Reaching out for help,
To drive away our woe.
How we look to God for Mercy
When there is much pain.
Seeking strength to struggle on
To weather all the rain.
There is none but God in Heaven
Gives us courage to go on.
He gives help and faith,
When all earthly hope is gone.
If anyone ever doubted
That there is a God above,
Let them listen to the pleadings
Of the ones who need His love.
Oct 1956
Sun Mon Tue Wed Thu Fri Sat
1 2 3 4 5 6
7 8 9 10 11 12 13
14 15 16 17 18 19 20
21 22 23 24 25 26 27
28 29 30 31

October
1956

Mercy

How we mortals look to Heaven
When the tide of life run low,
Reaching out for help
To drive away our woe.

How we look to God for mercy
When there is much pain.
Seeking strength to struggle on
To weather all the rain.

There is none but God in Heaven
Gives us courage to go on.
He gives help and faith
When all earthly hope is gone.

If anyone ever doubted
That there is a God above,
Let them listen to the pleadings
Of the ones who need His love.

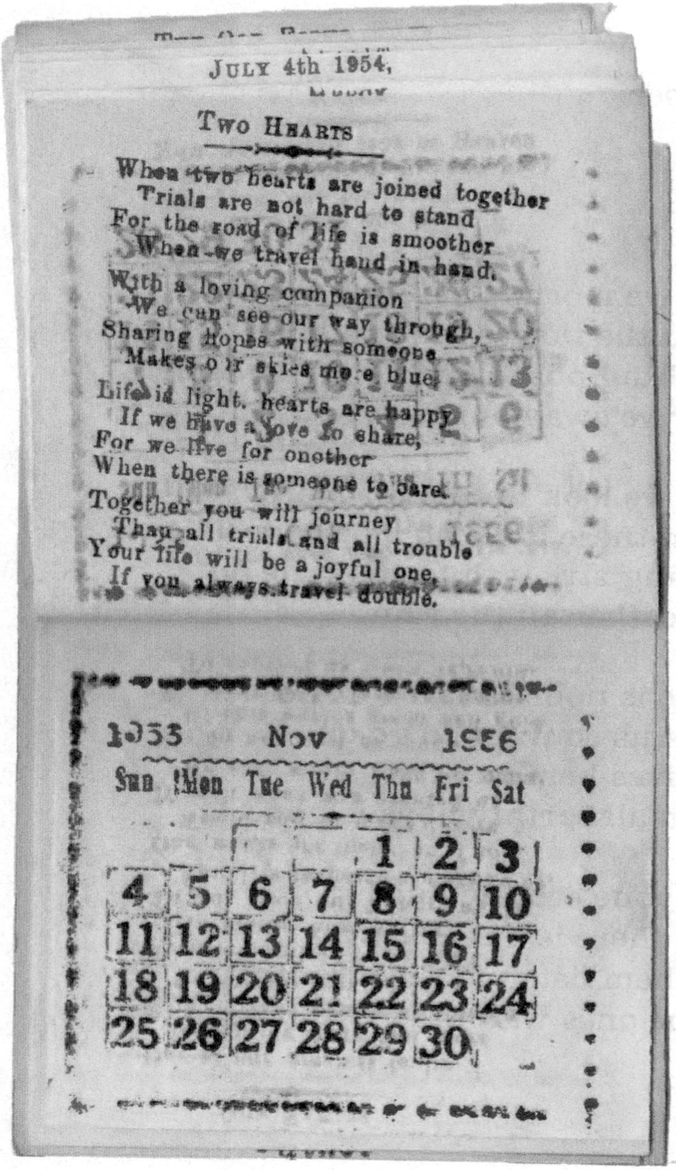
JULY 4th 1954,
TWO HEARTS
When two hearts are joined together
Trials are not hard to stand
For the road of life is smoother
When we travel hand in hand.
With a loving companion
We can see our way through,
Sharing hopes with someone
Makes our skies more blue.
Life is light, hearts are happy
If we have a love to share,
For we live for another
When there is someone to care.
Together you will journey
Than all trials and all trouble
Your life will be a joyful one,
If you always travel double.
Nov
1956
Sun Mon Tue Wed Thu Fri Sat
1 2 3
4 5 6 7 8 9 10
11 12 13 14 15 16 17
18 19 20 21 22 23 24
25 26 27 28 29 30

November
1956

Two Hearts

When two hearts are joined together
Trials are not hard to stand
For the road of life is smoother
When we travel hand in hand.

With a loving companion
We can see our way through.
Sharing hopes with someone
Makes our skies more blue.

Life is light, hearts are happy
If we have a love to share.
For we live for one another
When there is someone to care.

Together you will journey
Thru all trials and all trouble.
Your life will be a joyful one
If you always travel double.

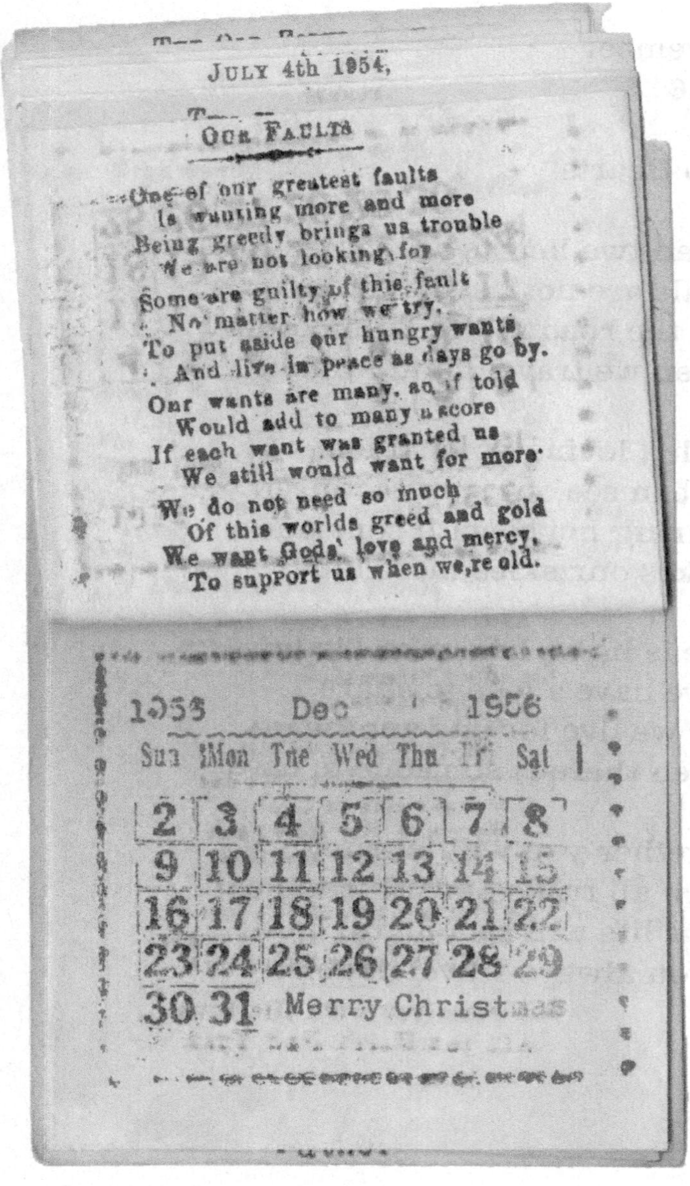
JULY 4th 1954,
OUR FAULTS
One of our greatest faults
Is wanting more and more
Being greedy brings us trouble
We are not looking for
Some are guilty of this fault
No matter how we try,
To put aside our hungry wants
And live in peace as days go by.
Our wants are many, so if told
Would add to many a score
If each want was granted us
We still would want for more
We do not need so much
Of this worlds greed and gold
We want Gods' love and mercy,
To support us when we,re old.
Dec 1956
Sun Mon Tue Wed Thu Fri Sat
2 3 4 5 6 7 8
9 10 11 12 13 14 15
16 17 18 19 20 21 22
23 24 25 26 27 28 29
30 31 Merry Christmas

December
1956

Our Faults

One of our greatest faults
Is wanting more and more.
Being greedy brings us trouble
We are not looking for.

Some are guilty of this fault
No matter how we try.
To put aside our hungry wants
And live in peace as days go by.

Our wants are many, so if told
Would add to many a score.
If each want was granted us
We still would want for more.

We do not need so much
Of this worlds greed and gold.
We want God's love and mercy
To support us when we're old.

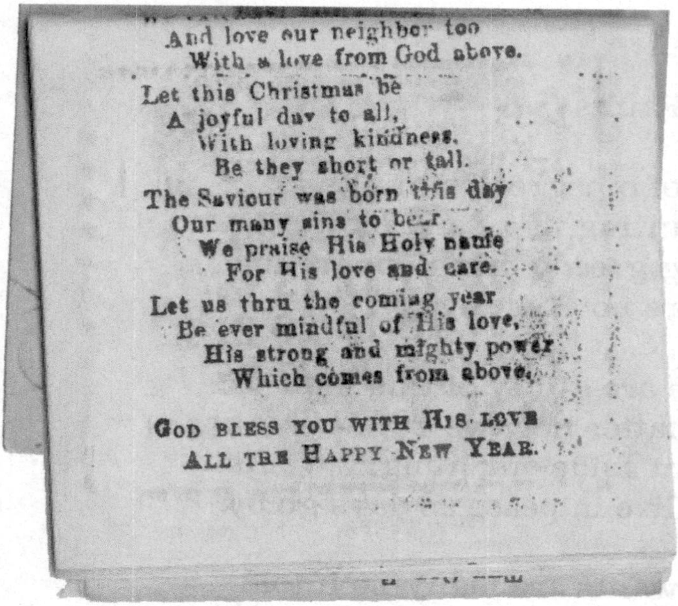

And love our neighbor too
With a love from God above.

Let this Christmas be
A joyful day to all,
With loving kindness,
Be they short or tall.
The Saviour was born this day
Our many sins to bear.
We praise His Holy name
For His love and care.
Let us thru the coming year
Be ever mindful of His love,
His strong and mighty power
Which comes from above.

GOD BLESS YOU WITH HIS LOVE
ALL THE HAPPY NEW YEAR.

This Christmas time
We extend kindred love
And love our neighbor too
With a love from God above

Let this Christmas be
A joyful day to all,
With loving kindness
Be they short or tall.

The Savior was born this day
Our many sins to bear.
We praise His Holy name
For His love and care.

Let us thru the coming year
Be ever mindful of His love,
His strong and mighty power
Which comes from above.

GOD BLESS YOU WITH HIS LOVE
ALL THE HAPPY NEW YEAR.

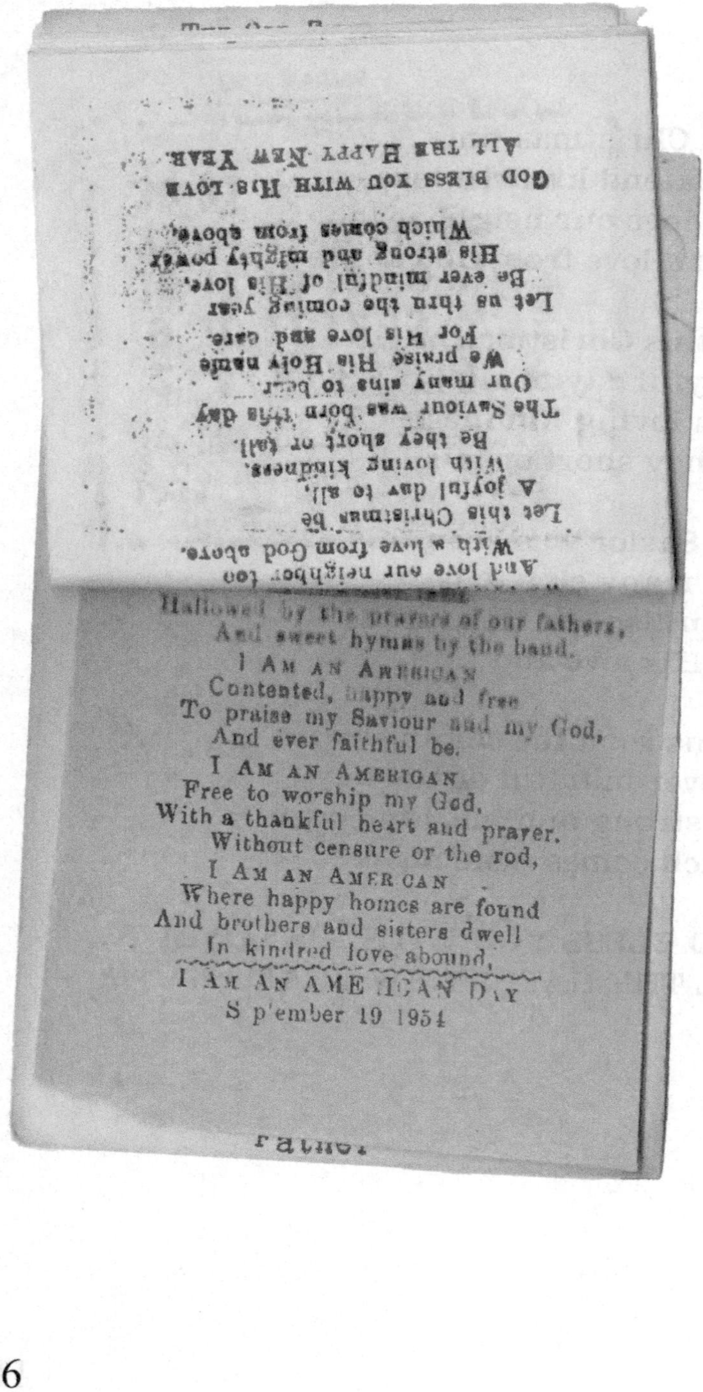
And love our neighbor too
With a love from God above.
Let this Christmas be
A joyful day to all,
With loving kindness,
Be they short or tall.
The Saviour was born this day
Our many sins to bear.
We praise His Holy name
For His love and care.
Let us thru the coming year
Be ever mindful of His love,
His strong and mighty power
Which comes from above.
God bless you with His love
All the Happy New Year.

Hallowed by the prayers of our fathers,
And sweet hymns by the band.
I Am an American
Contented, happy and free
To praise my Saviour and my God,
And ever faithful be.
I Am an American
Free to worship my God,
With a thankful heart and prayer,
Without censure or the rod,
I Am an Amer can
Where happy homes are found
And brothers and sisters dwell
In kindred love abound,
I Am An Ame ican Day
S p'ember 19 1954

I Am an American
In God's own free land
Hallowed by the prayers of our fathers,
And sweet hymns by the band,

I Am an American
Contented, happy and free
To praise my Savior and my God,
And ever faithful be.

I Am an American
Free to worship my God,
With a thankful heart and prayer,
Without censure or the rod.

I Am an American
Where happy homes are found
And brothers and sisters dwell
In kindred love abound.

I Am an American
September 19, 1951

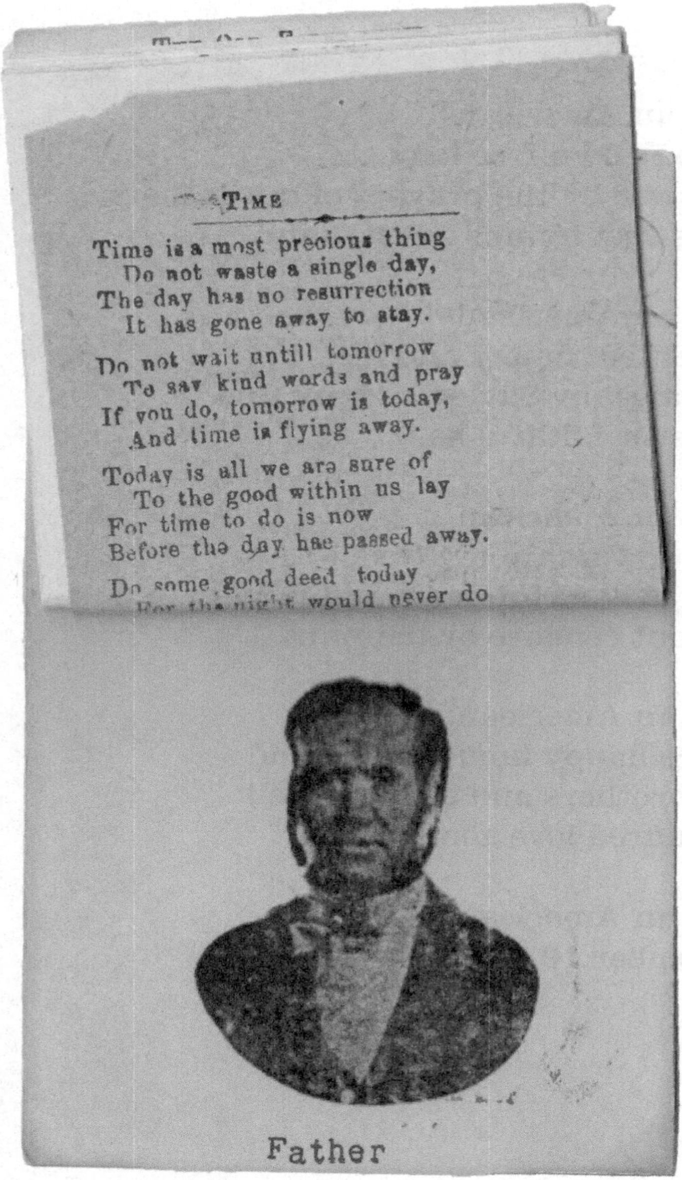
TIME
Time is a most precious thing
Do not waste a single day,
The day has no resurrection
It has gone away to stay.
Do not wait untill tomorrow
To say kind words and pray
If you do, tomorrow is today,
And time is flying away.
Today is all we are sure of
To the good within us lay
For time to do is now
Before the day has passed away.
Do some good deed today
Father

This is an actual photo of U.S. Moore's father, William.

Time

Time is a most precious thing
Do not waste a single day.
The day has no resurrection.
It has gone away to stay.

Do not wait until tomorrow
to say kind words and pray.
If you do, tomorrow is today,
And time is flying away.

Today is all we are sure of
To the good within us lay.
For time to do is now
Before the day has passed away.

Do some good deed today
For the night would never do
Do today, as you would have
Other folks do to you.

This is a photo of the actual house where U.S. Moore was born in January 30, 1865.

Made in the USA
Middletown, DE
16 August 2024

59200642R00080